Le handicap

Texte de Stéphanie Ledu
Illustrations de Laurent Richard

MiLAN

Certaines personnes entendent, voient, réfléchissent, marchent... Leur corps fonctionne normalement. Mais ce n'est pas le cas pour tout le monde.

Quelqu'un de notre famille, un ami, un voisin...
Nous connaissons tous des **gens handicapés**.
Cela veut dire qu'il y a des choses qu'ils ne peuvent pas faire, ou qu'ils font difficilement.

Vivre avec un handicap rend la vie compliquée ! Luc ne peut pas marcher, il se déplace en **fauteuil**. Zut ! impossible d'aller voir ce film : la salle de cinéma se trouve en haut d'un escalier et il n'y a pas d'ascenseur...

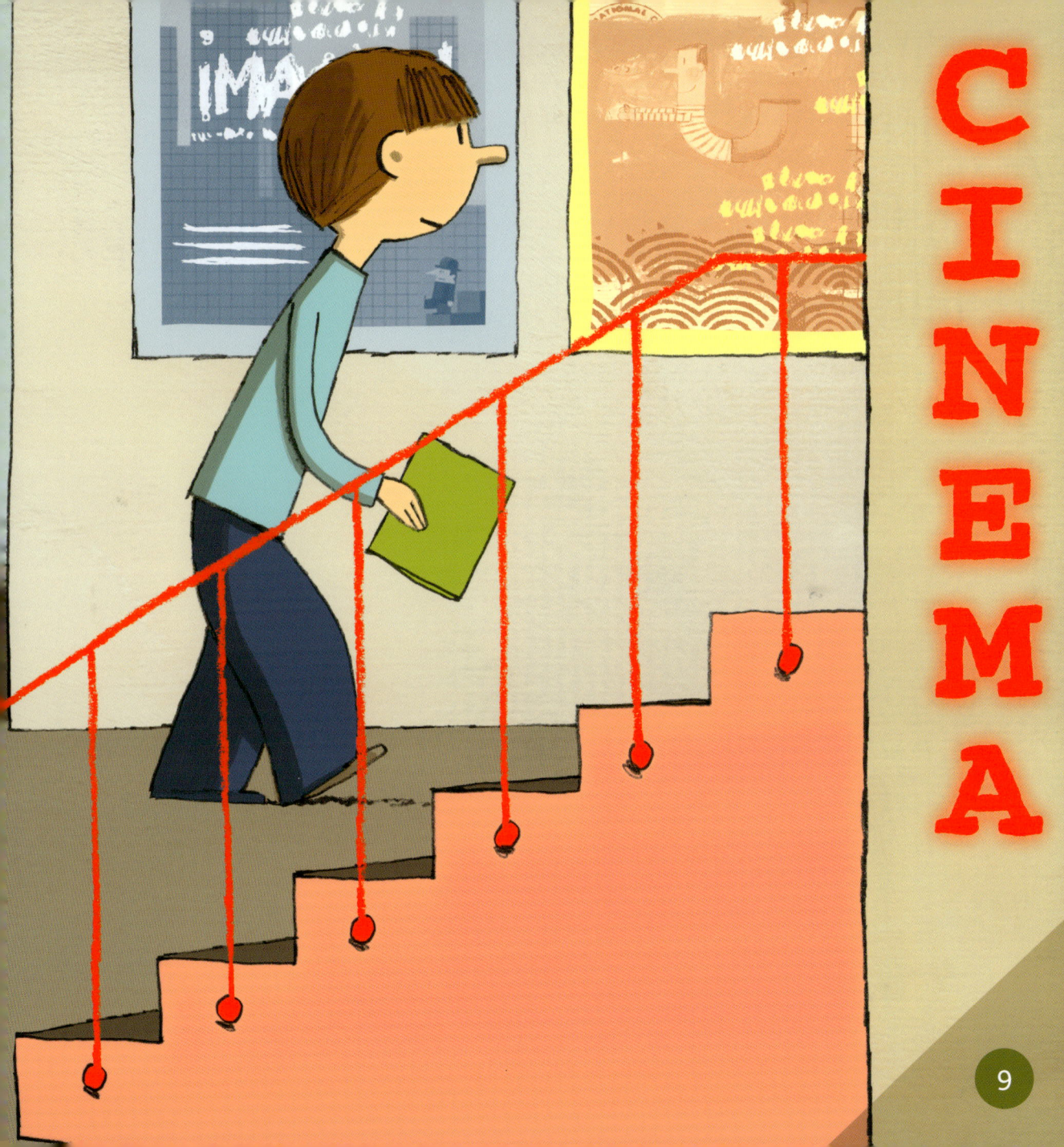

La voiture de Luc est adaptée pour qu'il puisse conduire. Elle possède un **macaron**, qui montre qu'il peut **stationner** sur les places réservées.

Mais parfois, des gens sans handicap s'y garent... Luc doit alors aller plus loin, faire plus de chemin : cela rend ses **déplacements** difficiles !

Anne ne voit pas : elle est **aveugle**.
Son chien l'aide à se diriger dans les rues.
Mais comment savoir si le bus qu'elle entend
arriver est celui qu'elle doit prendre ?

Jean est sourd : il n'entend pas et ne parle pas. Pour communiquer, il fait des gestes avec les mains. « Bonjour ! » Mais très peu de gens connaissent la langue des signes. C'est dommage...

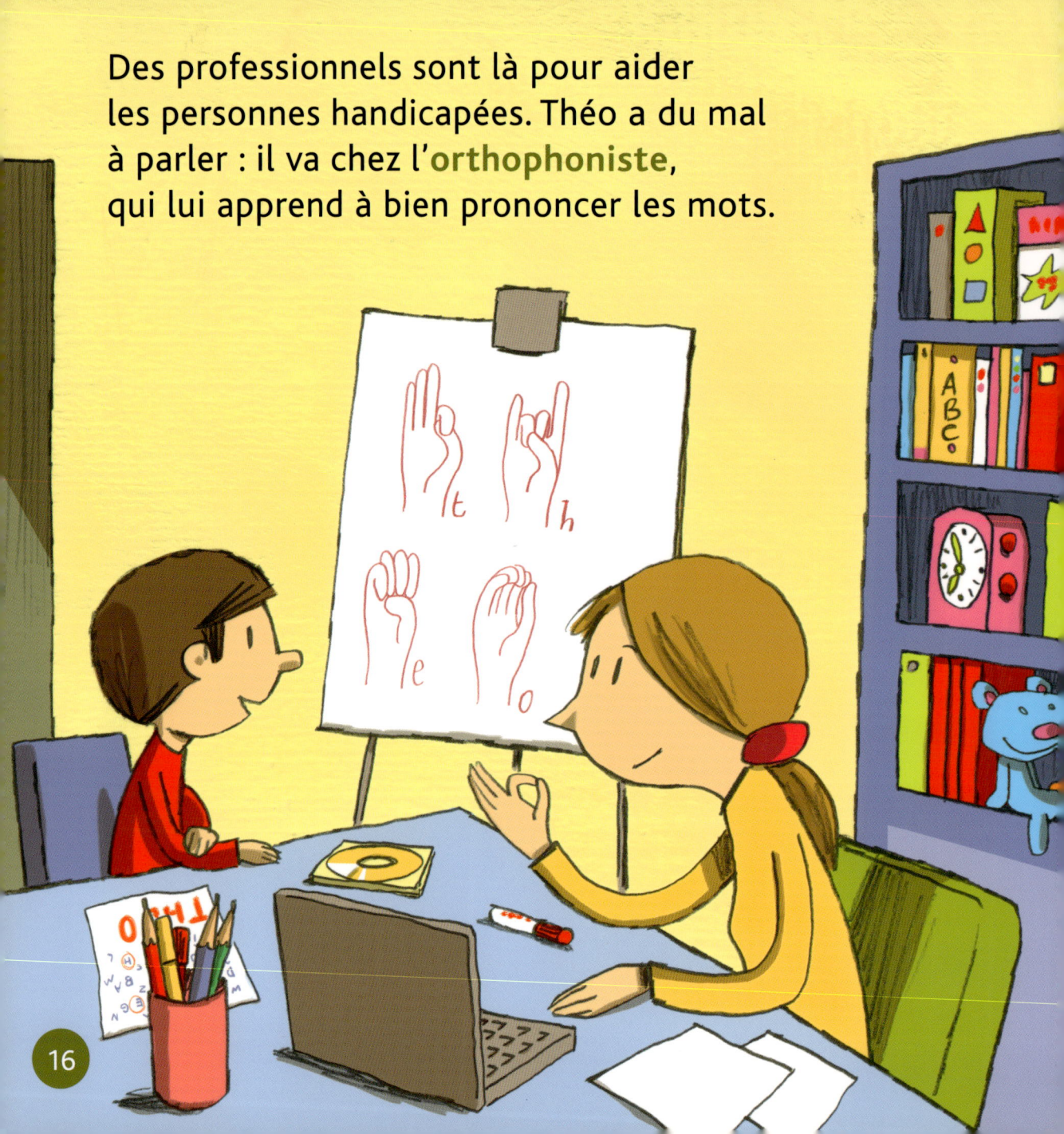

Des professionnels sont là pour aider les personnes handicapées. Théo a du mal à parler : il va chez l'**orthophoniste**, qui lui apprend à bien prononcer les mots.

Lou a eu un accident.
Le **kinésithérapeute** masse ses jambes.

Dans ce **centre de rééducation**, l'**ergothérapeute** réapprend à des personnes accidentées des gestes simples : marcher, s'habiller, se laver ou manger... Pour y arriver, il leur faut parfois beaucoup de **courage** !

Ces **sportifs handicapés** participent à une **compétition handisport**. Comme les autres champions, ils réalisent de véritables exploits sportifs !

Souvent, le handicap fait **peur** : certains sont gênés ou disent des choses méchantes... C'est bête. Cela fait du mal à la personne handicapée et à ceux qui l'aiment.

On ne choisit pas d'être handicapé ! Une minuscule anomalie dans le corps de Léna l'a fait naître trisomique. Elle a appris à parler et à marcher plus tard que les autres enfants...

Léna à 12 mois

Léna à 22 mois

Aujourd'hui, Léna va à l'école. Elle ne comprend pas tout aussi vite que ses copains, mais ils le savent et ils l'attendent. Dans la classe, un **auxiliaire** est aussi là pour l'aider.

Léna est d'abord Léna : certains jours rigolote et gentille, d'autres jours agaçante et un peu chipie...
Comme tous les enfants !

Découvre tous les titres de la collection

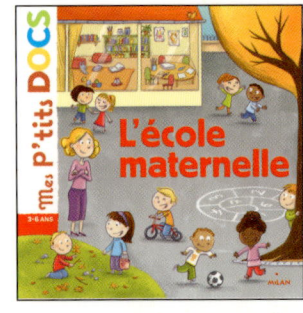
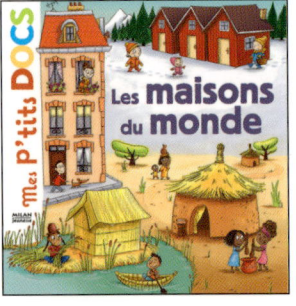

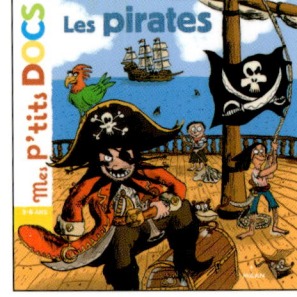

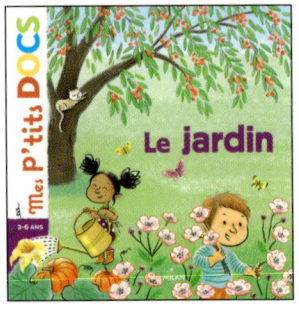

À table !
Au bureau
Les bateaux
Le bébé
Le bricolage
Les camions
Le chantier
Les châteaux forts

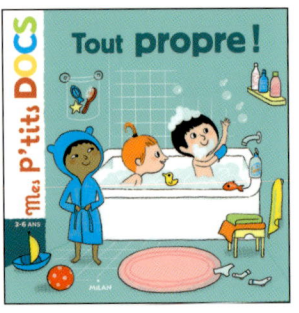

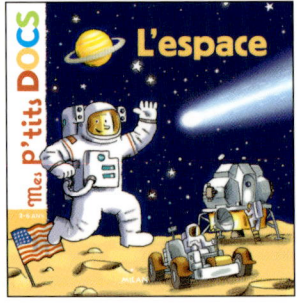

KRIEGSMARINE

A Pictorial History of the German Navy 1935-1945

by Robert C. Stern

illustrated by Don Greer
and Robert C. Stern

squadron/signal publications

(Cover) As the sun sets on 10 March 1941, *U124* prepares to get underway to resume hunting the sealanes off Freetown, leaving her meeting with *Scharnhorst* (Left) and *Gneisenau*. The battleships were nearing the end of Operation 'Berlin', the most successful of the Kriegsmarine's commerce raiding sorties.

If you have photographs of the aircraft, armor, soldiers or ships of any nation, particularly wartime snapshots, why not share them with us and help make Squadron/Signal's books all the more interesting and complete in the future. Any photograph sent to us will be copied and the original returned. The donor will be fully credited for any photos used. Please send them to: Squadron/Signal Publications Inc., 1115 Crowley Dr., Carrollton, TX 75006.

COPYRIGHT ©1979 by SQUADRON/SIGNAL PUBLICATIONS, INC.
1115 CROWLEY DR., CARROLLTON, TEXAS 75006

All rights reserved. No part of this publication may be reproduced, stored in a retrieval system, or transmitted in any form by any means electrical, mechanical or otherwise, without first seeking the written permission of the publisher.

ISBN 0-89747-094-X

Acknowledgements

The coverage in this book is consciously weighted largely in favor of the surface fleet units of the Kriegsmarine at the expense of U-boats. This is not because of any lack of appreciation for the contribution of the U-boat arm. Quite the opposite. It is because I feel that a book of this nature and size can't do justice to both, and since I intend to return to U-boats again in the future, this effort deliberately concentrates on the large surface units of the Kriegsmarine. Also I have consciously given no coverage to the preparations for Operation 'Sealion.' It is my belief that Hitler never intended to proceed with the invasion of England, that it was a propaganda bluff to delude the British and Russians. While the Kriegsmarine devoted much staff time and effort to 'Sealion', it didn't interfere with the activities of the major fleet units and therefore doesn't enter the scope of this book. Likewise the naval conflict in the Mediterranean, which involved none of the Kriegsmarine's major units, will be given only the briefest coverage.

I would like to thank the following without whom this book could never have been:

Bob Cressman
Dennis Smoke
Ken Macpherson
Jerry Beck
John Albrecht
Charles Haberlein
Ernst Schmidt

The above have assisted me in obtaining photos, have helped me with their personal recollections or have offered sound advice and criticism. However, any opinions expressed are mine alone and any factual errors which may have crept in are solely my responsibility.

The direct quotes from Grand Admiral Dönitz are all from his "The Conduct of the War at Sea", an essay delivered to the US Navy's Office of Naval Intelligence and published on 15 January 1946.

The color in the plates is based on English and German language sources and on the memory of Kriegsmarine veterans. Nevertheless some of the color has resulted from photo interpretation, a form of witchcraft. I invite any who agree or disagree to write me care of the publisher.

This book too is dedicated to Pat, whose absence during the period when most of this book was written forced me to find something else to fill my time, and to my father for bequeathing me the stubbornness to see it through under sometimes trying circumstances.

Photo Credits

Bundesarchiv Koblenz
Etablissement Cinematographique et Photographique des Armees (ECPA)
US National Archives and Record Service (NARS)
Naval Historical Center-US Navy (NHC)
Public Archives Canada
Bob Cressman
Ernst Schmidt
Ken Macpherson
John Albrecht

Operation 'Cerberus', the Channel Dash, was the ending to the most dramatic period of the war for the Kriegsmarine. On 12 February 1942 *Gneisenau* (Center), *Scharnhorst* (Right) and *Prinz Eugen* left the increasingly dangerous port of Brest for home waters by way of the shortest, most hazardous route. The move succeeded beyond any expectations, all ships reaching port safely. At the same time it marked the retreat of the Kriegsmarine from the Atlantic, the end of its most direct challenge to the Royal Navy. (Bundesarchiv)

The Prewar Years 1935-39

Except for a scratch force of pre-dreadnought battleships, ageing light cruisers and light forces, the once proud Imperial German Navy ceased to exist in November 1918. The battleships and battlecruisers that had repeatedly been reported sunk in battle by the British lay rotting on the seabed at Scapa Flow, scuttled by their own crews. Except for those few surviving old units, the Kriegsmarine, the German Navy of World War II, was a completely new entity. This fact was to be both the greatest strength and weakness of the reborn Kriegsmarine.

Starting anew, the Kriegsmarine was by 1939 equipped with warships which were newer and more efficient than those of her potential adversaries. The cruisers and battleships then entering service were among the finest ever designed, well armed and armored, fast and maneuverable. There were some technical weaknesses that could be blamed directly on the long hiatus in capital ship construction, particularly in the area of propulsion. But the greatest problem caused by the defeat and dismemberment of the Imperial German Navy was that the Kriegsmarine entered World War II with too few major units to ever seriously challenge the Royal Navy's command of the sea.

This situation need not have been. When Hitler renounced the military provisions of the Versailles Treaty in 1935, the Kriegsmarine was already expanding well beyond the limits of that treaty. The battleships **Scharnhorst** and **Gneisenau** had already been laid down and the heavy cruisers **Admiral Hipper** and **Blücher** had been ordered. This was on top of the five 'legal' light cruisers and three Panzerschiffe (literally, "armored ships", called "pocket battleships" by the British but never by the Germans, who later redesignated them as heavy cruisers) and 16 large destroyers built or being completed. The 1935 program called for a further massive expansion including the battleship **Bismarck**, aircraft carrier **Graf Zeppelin,** heavy cruiser **Prinz Eugen,** six more destroyers and 12 torpedo boats. It was an ambitious program augmented a year later by the ordering of an additional battleship, another aircraft carrier, two more heavy cruisers and numerous lighter forces. Unfortunately this promising start to naval rearmament wasn't followed through with the same energy with which it was started.

There were a number of reasons for this failure, some of which could be laid directly to the Navy. The general rearmament of Germany meant that supplies of metal and manpower that could have hastened completion of the ordered ships and boats were often diverted to other areas. Grand Admiral Erich Raeder wasn't able to alter the national priorities which gave the Luftwaffe and Army better access to vital resources. In part this was due to Raeder's personality and in part due to Hitler's. Raeder never was an infighter. He couldn't compete with such heavyweights as Göring in the byzantine court surrounding Hitler. Yet it was success in just that environment which often determined which projects were completed and which not. Complicating Raeder's problems was the fact that Hitler wasn't a seaman. He hated boats, having a tendency toward seasickness even on calm days, and didn't understand the uses of seapower. Like many largely self-taught men, he distrusted that which he didn't understand. He did know that prior to World War I vast sums had been spent on von Tirpitz' High Seas Fleet which had been ultimately wasted. And he knew that after it had spent the last two years of that war almost totally inactive, that magnificent fleet had become a hotbed of communist agitation. The 1918 fleet mutiny led directly to the collapse of Imperial Germany. All of this led Hitler to give ship building a low priority during the feverish pre-war rearmament.

A further delaying factor was the slowness with which the designs for these new cruisers and battleships were completed. This was caused in part by a lack of decision by SKL (Seekriegsleitung – Naval Staff) as to the exact purpose to which these new units were to be put. Were they to be independent commerce raiders or were they to form part of a homogeneous battle squadron? When hard choices had to be made between armament and protection, speed and endurance, the decisions were often delayed and confused. The argument was never really settled, factions in the fleet supporting either position, forcing compromises in many of the designs. As a result, some of the new ships ended up ideally suited for neither task. Most obvious were the problems with the Hipper-type heavy cruisers which were too short-ranged to act as independent raiders, too lightly armored to have much hope in a battleline, and yet they were much larger, faster and more powerful than they needed to be to act as convoy escorts, minelayers or patrol vessels, typical uses for shorter-ranged cruisers.

One of the handful of pre-dreadnought battleships allowed the Reichsmarine by the Versailles Treaty is seen passing through the Kaiser Wilhelm Canal. *Schleswig-Holstein* **and** *Schlesien* **were taken in hand for major refit in 1935 but no amount of refitting could turn them into modern warships, adequate to needs of a rearming Germany. (NARS)**

The argument came to a head in 1938. After years of repeated assurances that there was no need to fear another confrontation with England, and years of repeated warnings by Raeder that to enter a conflict with England without a much stronger Navy would doom the Kriegsmarine to sure failure, Hitler reversed himself in May 1938 and declared England the main enemy. He demanded that a plan for massive naval expansion be developed and implemented as quickly as possible, with 1945 as the target date. There began months of heated discussion over what size and shape of fleet would be ideal. All the admirals and their staffs were products of the old Imperial Navy. All were determined that the humiliating bottling-up of Germany's fleet would never happen again. The only question was how. There were a few voices that called for a basic alteration of strategy to suit Germany's unique geography. The head of the tiny U-boat arm, Karl Dönitz, saw the very geography that had hobbled the High Seas Fleet in World War I as an advantage.

> ... a direct attack by enemy fleets in German home waters was not to be expected, because of our strength in the air and the forces available on the coast, so all sections of the German Fleet were free for offensive action.

Along with a core of younger staff officers, Dönitz claimed that the idea of battlefleet confrontations was obsolete. No longer could command of the sea be determined by the outcome of a single great battle. Only by denying England the free passage of her merchant fleet could her existence be threatened.

England was in every respect dependent on sea-borne supply for food and import of raw materials, as well as for development of every type of military power. The single task of the German Navy was, therefore, to interrupt or cut these sea communications. It was clear that this object could never be obtained by building a fleet to fight the English Fleet and in this way win the sea communications. The only remaining method was to attack sea communications quickly . . . When the focus of the war at sea was turned to shipping, it was obvious that, as far as possible, the surface forces had to be devoted to this task as well. Here only was there a chance for the Navy to play an important, perhaps even decisive, part in the general conduct of the war.

Obviously Dönitz thought that his U-boats were the most ideally suited for the task of commerce raiding, but even he wouldn't have argued against the necessity of a surface fleet to balance the attack. But nobody asked his opinion. He wasn't even invited to speak to the group of eight flag and staff officers who were given the task of drawing up the Kriegsmarine's new building plans. The closest any came to dissenting from the prevailing inclination to recommend the construction of a massive battlefleet were the fleet commander Hermann Boehm and staff planner Hellmuth Heye who argued that perhaps commerce raiding would be decisive in any future war. Both also saw that U-boats were well suited to the task of commerce raiding and had to be available in large numbers to be effective. But Boehm wasn't a member of the committee and Heye felt that technical improvements in ASW (Anti-Submarine Warfare) had limited the usefulness of U-boats, and that surface raiders would be more effective in disrupting England's commerce. In the end, the majority of old-line Admirals prevailed and the 'Z'-Plan (for Ziel-target) was submitted to Hitler in January 1939.

The plan called for the fleet to comprise, by 1945, ten battleships (**Bismarck** and **Tirpitz, Scharnhorst** and **Gneisenau** which were to be converted to 38cm (15″) main armament and six new H-type), six P-type 'Super **Deutschland**' 28cm (11″) heavy cruisers plus five **Hipper**-type 20cm (8″) heavy cruisers, two aircraft carriers, five light cruisers, 50 destroyers and 229 U-boats.

Hitler enthusiastically approved the 'Z'-Plan on 29 January 1939 with the words: "For my political aims I shall not need the fleet before 1946". It would have been a fleet well suited to refighting World War I. The lack of emphasis on carrier-borne airpower is incomprehensible and anachronistic, and probably would have been disastrous. But the fleet never had a chance to prove its worth because the outbreak of war in 1939 found only the first keels laid for the major new units of the 'Z'-Plan. The Kriegsmarine would have to fight the war with those ships that had been ordered in 1936 and before, and many of those were far from

The first new warships designed and built for the Reichsmarine were two classes of torpedo boats, the Type 1923, named after birds of prey (Raubvogel) and the Type 1924, named after hunting animals (Raubtier). (Above) A Type 1923 boat, probably *Greif,* is seen in harbor during the 1929 fleet maneuvers. For those maneuvers, torpedo boats carried a temporary medium gray and black splinter camouflage. In the right foreground is the bow of the new light cruiser *Königsberg.* (Bob Cressman) (Below) Two Type 1924 torpedo boats, *Jaguar* and *Tiger,* break the battleline in front of two pre-dreadnought battleships. They are painted in the more normal pre-war torpedo boat livery of overall black. (NARS)

Three pre-dreadnought battleships are seen in harbor in 1935. *Schleswig-Holstein* is in the foreground, *Schlesien* to the left and *Hessen* in the background. The major external difference in the refitted ships is the trunking together of the two foremost funnels. (NHC)

complete. **Bismarck, Tirpitz, Graf Zeppelin, Blücher** and **Prinz Eugen** had all been launched but wouldn't be ready for months or years. The battle fleet of September 1939 comprised only **Gneisenau, Admiral Hipper, Admiral Graf Spee, Deutschland,** five light cruisers and 22 destroyers. **Scharnhorst** and **Admiral Scheer** were in dock. The situation in U-boat command was even more bleak. By scraping the bottom of the barrel, just 21 sea-going U-boats were available for operations off the coast of England.

The fleet that prepared in early September 1939 to face the veteran Royal Navy was largely untried and unproved. It had been seasoned only by some peacetime cruises and a few scuffles with Spanish Republican aircraft in 1937. England, France, Italy and Germany had responded to the outbreak of civil war in Spain with many high-sounding phrases about 'Big Power' neutrality. But while the British and French appeared to intend honestly to maintain strict neutrality, perhaps hoping that the whole mess would quickly blow over, the Germans and Italians used the neutrality agreements to cover continued assistance to the Nationalist side. Each nation maintained warships off a sector of the Spanish coast on the so-called Neutrality Patrol, to restrict the flow of contraband. Most of the warships of the infant Kriegsmarine participated at some time between 1936 and 1938. Spanish Republican frustration at a 'Neutrality Patrol' that restricted the import of arms to them but not the other side finally boiled over in spring 1937. On 29 May, Republican aircraft attacked **Deutschland** off Ibiza, obtaining two hits. Responding quickly, two days later **Admiral Scheer** shelled the Republican port city of Almeira. Both sides apparently felt that honor had been satisfied and that nothing further could be gained. There were no further incidents.

Small units of the fleet were employed again on 23 March 1939, to carry troops to Memel, an ex-East Prussian city being repossessed by Hitler.

When European tensions began to heighten again in the fall of 1939, spurred on by Hitler's demands against Poland, the Kriegsmarine reluctantly made increasing preparations for war. In August leaves were cancelled and refits hurried to speed completion. The pre-dreadnought battleship **Schleswig-Holstein** had already been sent to Danzig as part of Hitler's muscle-flexing. Now, on 21 August, the heavy cruiser **Admiral Graf Spee** sailed through the English Channel enroute to the South Atlantic. Three days later **Deutschland** left Kiel for the North Atlantic. Both ships were under orders to 'get lost', avoiding contact with any other vessels until the danger passed or hostilities commenced. In the next few days the available sea-going U-boats left to take up their positions around England.

Still no one in the Kriegsmarine expected that war would really start in the fall of 1939. No one was psychologically prepared for war. Surely England and France would back down again as they had at Münich. Surely they wouldn't go to war over weak Poland after they had abandoned a much stronger ally in Czechoslovakia. But they did. The outbreak of war had caught the Kriegsmarine in the very trap of severe numerical inferiority which Raeder had wished so fervently to avoid. It is a moot point to discuss whether the 'Z'-Plan was a ruse by Hitler to deceive the British or whether he did expect Poland to fall without Allied intervention. Whatever Hitler's intentions may have been, the result was to thrust the Kriegsmarine into a war for which it simply wasn't prepared.

Visiting Shanghai in 1931, *Emden* **was the first of a series of 15cm (6″) cruisers that were the first large warships designed in Germany after World War I.** *Emden* **was basically similar to the large light cruisers that were being built at the end of that war, most noticeably in that she carried her main armament in single turrets. (NHC)**

Following *Emden* came three similar, larger light cruisers which carried their armament in triple turrets, one forward, two aft. (Above) The first of the series, *Karlsrühe*, is seen at Swinemünde sometime after November 1935 when the new Kriegsmarine ensign was adopted. (Left) Seen from a bridge across the Kaiser Wilhelm Canal, *Köln* shows the offset rear turrets characteristic of the class. This was done in an effort to give more forward arc to the primarily aft mounted main armament. The black circle on 'Bruno' turret was an air recognition mark. (NHC) (Below) *Königsberg* is seen in 1934, during the transitional period between the Reichsmarine and Kriegsmarine. The Nazis have come to power as can be attested by the swastika and eagle on the transom but the Reichsmarine ensign is still being flown. (Bob Cressman)

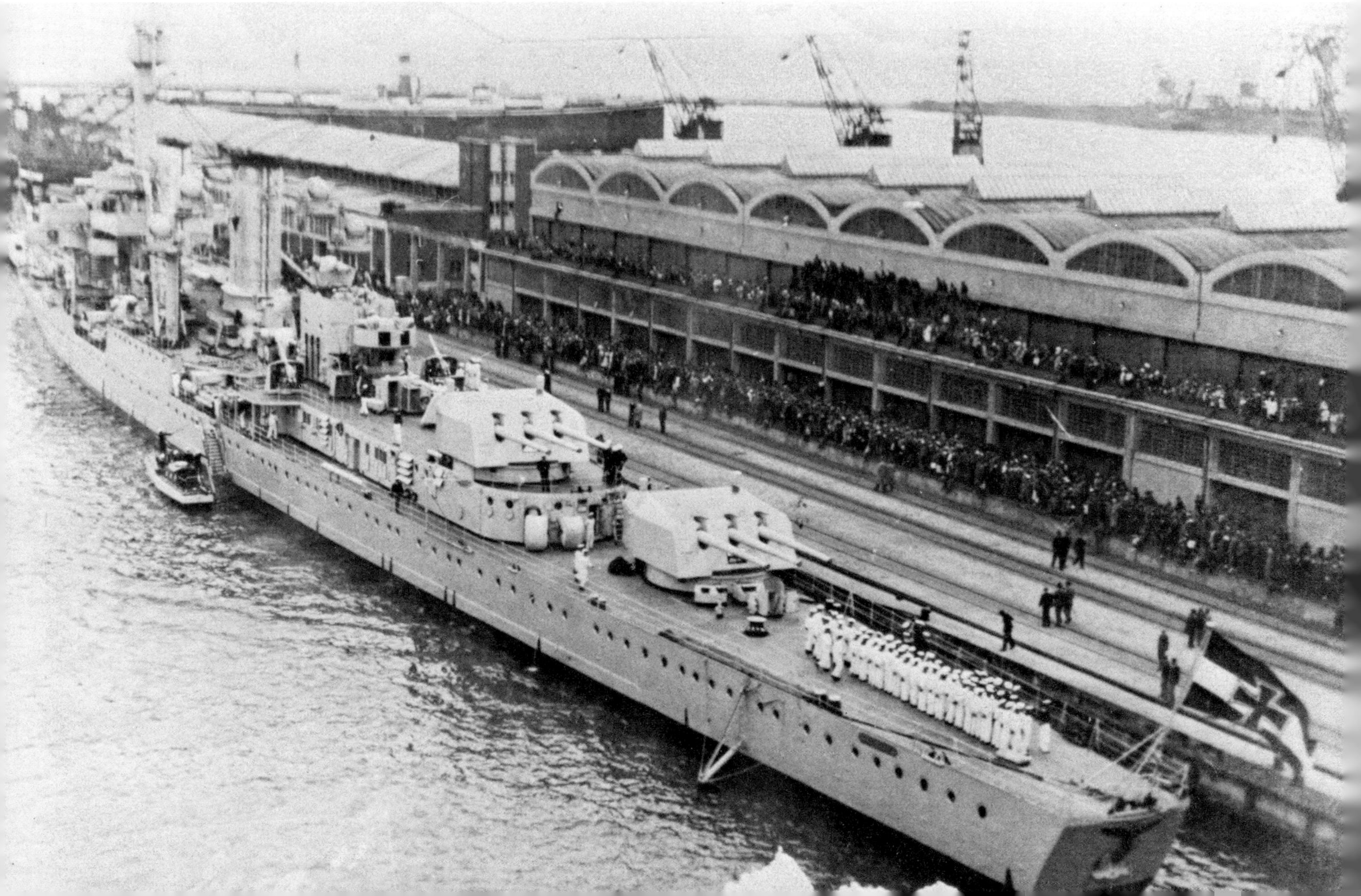

Two further ships completed the series of 15cm-armed cruisers. Near sisters, they could be distinguished from the three preceding ships by their single funnels. They were also beamier and their after turrets were carried on the centerline. *Leipzig* (Above) and *Nurnberg* (Below) were the most modern and efficient light cruisers available at the outbreak of the war, but they were too lightly armored and short ranged to be really useful. Bad luck kept them out of front line service for most of the war. (NHC)

In order to replace the oldest of her pre-dreadnoughts, Germany was allowed by the Versailles Treaty to build capital ships of up to 10,000 tons. Since the tonnage of a battleship of the day was at least three times that figure, this restriction was obviously intended to limit Germany to the construction of coast-defense ships. The design to which the three Panzerschiffe were built proved to be inspired, possibly the most original and successful surface ships of the Kriegsmarine. *Deutschland* (Above), *Admiral Scheer* (Below) and *Admiral Graf Spee* (Bottom) had two triple 28cm (11") turrets and diesel propulsion which gave them good speed and excellent range. The guiding principle was that they should be able to outfight any smaller ships and outrun any larger. While the advent of the fast battleship during the '30s invalidated part of that thesis, they nevertheless proved to be ideal commerce raiders. (NHC)

Totally banned by the Versailles Treaty, the U-boat arm, under Kapitän z.S. Karl Dönitz, came into clandestine existence in 1933 before being legitimized by the Anglo-German Naval Agreement of 1935. The first boats of the new force were small Type II coastal boats, intended primarily for training. (Above) *U1, U4, U2,* and *U3,* the first Type IIAs, muster their crews for Morning Colors. (NHC) (Left) Docked alongside the tender *Saar* at Scheer-Hafen, Kiel-Wick at least eight assorted Type IIs can be seen. *U19,* second from the left, carries an overall medium gray scheme with white numerals, while the remaining boats have light gray towers and black numbers. (Ernst Schmidt) (Below) Only gradually did the larger, sea-going Type VIIs arrive to augment the Type IIs. Here a Type VIIB is being put in commission at Germania Werft, Kiel during the hard winter of 1939-40. (Ken Macpherson)

In the 1930s the Kriegsmarine began to build large destroyers to supplement the earlier torpedo boats. They were large and well armed but suffered from poor range, inadequate sea-keeping and extremely temperamental high-pressure boilers. (Above) The first of the new destroyers, *Leberecht Maass (Z1)*, is being commissioned, 1937. (NARS) (Left & Right) Practice torpedoes from *Leberecht Maass* and *Erich Steinbrinck (Z15)* are seen during recovery. The red and white bands indicated a dummy warhead. (Bob Cressman) (Below) *Hans Lüdemann (Z18)* carries her flotilla designator in large, shadowed numbers on her side. '53' indicates that she was the third boat of the fifth flotilla. (NARS)

A small navy such as the Kriegsmarine depends even more on its small forces, the ships that do the unglamorous work of coastal protection, minelaying and sweeping, and convoy escort. (Left) *M6* leads three other 770 ton minesweepers in this 1939 view. These were handy boats which saw much service beyond their intended role. (NARS) (Above) *F2*, a 712 ton corvette, was designed specifically for convoy escort but wasn't particularly successful, being faster and shorter-ranged than necessary. (NARS) (Below Left) *S12* followed by two sisters comes alongside her tender. The S-boats, fast motor torpedo boats, were the most publicized and feared of the small forces. They saw action in all theaters, most particularly the English Channel. (NARS) (Below) The R-boats, such as *R29* seen here, were motor minesweepers that served with distinction in all functions, from sweepers to escort, sub chaser to picket boat, and more. (NARS)

For the most part the prewar years from 1935 to 1939 were peaceful ones for the Kriegsmarine, spent largely in training crews for the large, new ships expected to enter service shortly. (Above) Watched by a large, attentive audience, *Köln* fires a practice torpedo. A canvas awning protects her fantail from the summer sun. (NARS) (Left) Each Marineschule class spent at least six months on a round-the-world cruise. Here *Karlsrühe* stops at St. Thomas, Virgin Islands, 7 May 1936. (NHC) (Below) When not off cruising, Kriegsmarine ships would be receiving visitors from other navies on similar jaunts. At Kiel *Admiral Graf Spee* is seen from USS Wyoming, 1937. (NHC)

The Spanish Civil War and the four-power Neutrality Patrol brought the Kriegsmarine its first action and its first battle casualties. Most sea-worthy units of the Kriegsmarine saw some service with the Neutrality Patrol. The most visible vessels that could be deployed were the Panzerschiffe. *Admiral Scheer* (Above) is seen docked at Gibraltar, *Deutschland* (Left) is seen from a passing German passenger ship. Note the red, white and black bands on each main turret. Each of the four-powers carried a different color pattern of bands to identify its ships. As the most visible symbol of the German presence off Spain, *Deutschland* was the target of Republican bombers on 29 May 1937. She was hit twice, several seamen being killed. In reprisal, *Scheer* bombarded Almeira two days later. (NHC, NARS)

Reichsmarine Ensign

Kriegsmarine Ensign

Kriegsmarine Jack

Admiral's Flags

Admiral

Vice Admiral

Rear Admiral

Smaller units also participated in the Neutrality Patrol and carried the three-stripe marking. (Above) *Leipzig* is seen in 1938, passing the stern of *Schleswig-Holstein.* (NARS) (Right) *Möwe* is seen at sea in heavy weather off the coast of Spain. Torpedo boats have now changed over to the standard Kriegsmarine livery of medium gray hull and light gray superstructure. (Bob Cressman) (Below) *Deutschland* and three Type 1923 torpedo boats rest at Naples, the main port for German vessels serving off Spain. (NHC)

While the existing units of the Kriegsmarine were involved off Spain, the new construction of the 1934 and 1935 programs was being rushed to completion. (Above) *Gneisenau* was commissioned in May 1938, immediately becoming the new fleet flagship. As launched she carried two catapults, the main one with a He114, the turret catapult with an Ar95. (NHC) (Left) The experience of the British, Japanese and Americans had already pointed to the critical importance of naval airpower. In belated response to this the aircraft carrier *Graf Zeppelin* was launched on 8 December 1938, but inexperience in carrier design and disagreements as to her armament and aircraft led to delays in her completion. (Below) The Kriegsmarine's most ambitious design to date, the first 'real' battleship to be launched by Germany since 1917, *Bismarck* was launched with great fanfare on 14 February 1939. Note her straight stem, characteristic of all German capital ships to this point. (NHC)

Looking massive and powerful, two of Germany's new warships are seen immediately after their commissioning. Both have straight stems which made them very wet in rough weather and led to their conversion to 'Atlantic' clipper bows. (Above) *Scharnhorst*, sister to *Gneisenau*, is seen here between her commissioning in January 1939 and her conversion in July. (NHC) (Below) The first of the Kriegsmarine's new 20cm (8") heavy cruisers, *Admiral Hipper*, is seen in 1939. Her straight stem was modified before the outbreak of war. (Bundesarchiv)

As international tensions increased in 1939, the Kriegsmarine was placed on a war footing. (Above) Small units were used to transport troops for the occupation of Memel, 23 March 1939. *Leberecht Maass* is visible in the foreground, a second destroyer is to the left. *Wolf,* another torpedo boat and an M1-class minesweeper are in the left background. An earlier minesweeper is to the right. (Left) To commemorate the World War I victory at Tannenburg and also to position units for a possible invasion of Poland, troops and ships were sent to East Prussia. Among the ships sent was *Schleswig-Holstein,* seen arriving at Danzig. (NARS) (Below) As a precaution against hostilities with the West, the two Panzerschiffe (reclassed as heavy cruisers after the war began) then available were sent to sea in August, 1939. *Deutschland* sailed for a waiting area south of Greenland. *Admiral Graf Spee,* seen here passing through the English Channel, sailed for the South Atlantic. (Bob Cressman)

The Early Days,
September 1939 – March 1940

Hostilities began at dawn on 1 September 1939 when **Schleswig-Holstein** began shelling the Polish Westerplatte fortress across from Danzig. The shelling was in support of an abortive landing attempt. **Schleswig-Holstein** was the largest unit committed to the Polish campaign, three light cruisers also being assigned minelaying and troop transport duties. There was no significant opposition from the Polish Navy, the largest units of which, three new destroyers, had sailed for England a week earlier. The bulk of the Kriegsmarine waited in the west.

In spite of the tough language that had come from England in the past months, no one in Germany seemed to believe that war would result from their 'trouble' with Poland, least of all the Kriegsmarine which clung desperately to Hitler's assurance that the Western Allies would back down, that the fleet wouldn't be needed for years to come. When the realization finally came that war with England and France had indeed begun, the reaction at SKL was at first shock and then gloom. Dönitz' reaction was sorrow that he should again be fighting England, although he displayed confidence that his U-boats would be equal to the task. Raeder seemed more shaken. His mood at the time could best be described by an earlier statement: "If ever they (the fleet) have to struggle with the British, they would only be able to show that they could die with dignity.'

In spite of such dire predictions, the war at sea actually began rather slowly as neither side was really prepared. The first word that war with England had indeed begun came to German forces from an 'in clear' message monitored on the Royal Navy band sent at 1230 on 3 September 1939. Not until 1300 did SKL transmit its own confirmation: "Hostilities with Britain to be opened forthwith."

Within hours, the first controversial incident of the war had occurred. On the evening of 3 September Fritz-Julius Lemp of **U30** sighted and sank a ship he took for an armed merchant cruiser. In fact his victim was **Athenia**, a 13,500GRT liner carrying over 1400 passengers. Quick reaction by the Royal Navy managed to save all but 112 of those onboard, but the U-boat war was off to an unexpected start. The U-boats that ringed England that evening were actually under greater restraint than their counterparts of 1917 had been. SKL had decided definitely against unrestricted U-boat warfare. One reason was a desire to avoid just the kind of incident that had now occurred. Lemp's orders specifically required that he follow prize rules with all merchant or passenger ships not in convoy. These rules required that the U-boat had to surface, halt the intended victim with a shot across the bow, inspect her papers for nationality and, if a neutral, her cargo manifests for contraband, make adequate provision for the survival of her crew and only then sink her. The only exception to these rules were warships, which could be sunk without warning. Had **Athenia** indeed been an armed merchant cruiser, Lemp would have been within orders when he sank her.

Lemp's case of mistaken identity proved to be a great propaganda coup for the British. He maintained radio silence for several days after the incident. When British broadcasts began to mention this first 'atrocity', German radio denied it, claiming, and believing that the story was a fabrication. Only when Lemp reported in did the Germans realize that the British reports had been essentially accurate and that they had lost the first round of the propaganda 'war' and had lost important credibility with such powerful neutrals as the United States. More importantly this incident began the process which led inevitably to unrestricted U-boat warfare. With the sinking of **Athenia**, the Royal Navy had to assume that such a state existed already and began arming all merchant vessels. The Germans, on the other hand, reacted by restricting their U-boats even more tightly, for instance, forbidding the sinking of passenger ships even in convoy. In the same vein permission for **Deutschland** and **Graf Spee** to begin operations was delayed, orders for the ships to remain hidden staying in effect. This trend toward greater restriction couldn't continue. All British merchant ships were ordered to begin transmitting the "SS" warning signal whenever stopped by a U-boat, which was in violation of prize rules. Those rules dated from a century earlier, before the invention of either submarines or radios. Inevitably the restrictions on U-boat operations were progressively relaxed and, by the end of the year, totally abolished. On 26 September, permission was finally granted to the two cruisers at sea to begin operations.

On the second day of the hostilities, 4 September, the British set the tone for their reaction to the threat posed by the Kriegsmarine. The RAF launched bombing raids on **Scharnhorst** and **Gneisenau** at Brunsbüttel and on **Admiral Scheer** at Wilhelmshaven. The raids weren't well coordinated nor large but succeeded in surprising the German defenses and nearly succeeded in inflicting great damage. Two 500lb. bombs hit **Scheer** but bounced off her deck without exploding. These initial raids weren't followed up by others for some time. Nevertheless they should have signalled to SKL the immense threat that British airpower represented. More of the Kriegsmarine's warships were to be lost to that cause than any other.

After such an exciting start the war soon settled into a routine. Except for the largest units, which were kept at readiness at North Sea ports, nearly all other German warships were employed in laying the 'Westwall' mine barrage in the Heligoland Bight. Only at the end of the month did

Schleswig-Holstein opened hostilities at dawn on 1 September 1939 by firing on the Polish Westerplatte fortress opposite Danzig. The bombardment was to cover a marine landing which failed to capture the fort. (Bob Cressman)

The outbreak of war with England took the Kriegsmarine by surprise, filling many with foreboding. Here the off-duty crew is gathered on the afterdeck of one of the K-class cruisers as the CPO reads the declaration of war. (ECPA)

the Kriegsmarine take the offensive on the surface. The two raiding cruisers were finally unleashed. **Graf Spee** had her first success on 30 September, sinking the 5,000GRT freighter **Clement** near Pernambuco, Brazil. **Deutschland** claimed her first victim on 10 October, capturing an American steamer carrying contraband on the Halifax route.

The appearance of these raiders on essential shipping lanes had the desired result. Shipping was rerouted or delayed. Naval groups were formed to hunt for the raiders, drawing Royal Navy capital ships away from England. This presented the Germans with an excellent opportunity to confront the Royal Navy's cruiser blockade which was rapidly decimating Germany's merchant fleet. On 7 October, **Gneisenau** and **Köln** (**Scharnhorst** was in dock with boiler trouble) sailed from Germany toward the coast of Norway in an attempt to drag Royal Navy pursuit over a line of U-boats. This was identical to several German operations in the First World War including that which resulted in the battle of Jutland. Predictably, the operation was a failure. The British saw the potential trap and attacked only with aircraft. No hits were obtained by the RAF and all ships returned unharmed. Incredibly, major units of the fleet had been risked on a 20 year old plan and a wonderful opportunity wasted. Nothing could better show the unfortunate inability of SKL to react to a new, advantageous situation. The Kriegsmarine was paying the price for its lack of preparation.

A number of improvements had occurred in the situation of the Kriegsmarine before SKL was ready to directly challenge the British blockade. Luftwaffe and U-boat attacks had forced the removal of the Royal Navy's main anchorage from Scapa Flow to Loch Ewe on the west coast of Scotland. As if to punctuate the wisdom of this move, on the night of 13-14 October, **U47** under Gunther Prien crept into Scapa Flow and sank the old battleship **Royal Oak.** Three days later, Kriegsmarine destroyers began a program of offensive mining along the English coast using an improved magnetic mine. In 11 operations between then and February 1940, 17 of Germany's 22 operational destroyers laid minefields that accounted for 67 merchant ships of 252,000GRT, three destroyers and six auxilliary warships. None of the intruding destroyers was damaged during these operations. In early November, the heavy cruiser **Deutschland**, having had little success in the North Atlantic, was recalled. She succeeded in dodging the blockade, docking at Gotenhafen (Gdynia) on 17 November.

Only on 21 November, **Scharnhorst** being considered again ready for operations, did SKL plan a sortie against the Northern Patrol. The plan called for **Scharnhorst** and **Gneisenau** to attempt to 'roll up' the cruiser line between the Faroes and Iceland and to feint a breakout into the Atlantic, thereby relieving pressure on **Graf Spee.** In the late afternoon of 23 November, southeast of Iceland, **Scharnhorst** encountered the armed merchant cruiser **HMS Rawalpindi.** Three minutes after **Scharnhorst** opened fire **Rawalpindi** was burning and in another ten had sunk. For two hours the two battleships remained on the scene picking up survivors. When a warship was seen approaching out of the dark at high speed, the new fleet commander, Admiral Marschall, ordered his ships underway. Under a smokescreen laid by **Scharnhorst** the two battleships fled to the northeast in the face of a single British cruiser. A few hours later 'B' Service, the Kriegsmarine's radio intelligence unit, informed Marschall that the British cruiser had mistakenly informed the Admiralty that the battleships were headed southeast, back to Germany. This mistake ruined the effectiveness of the feigned breakout as the Royal Navy assumed the battleships were headed home. Continuing to the northeast, Marschall went into hiding, hoping to reappear when the hue and cry had died down. Rapidly deteriorating weather, however, did indeed make conditions favorable for a return home. In spite of the presence of six British and French capital ships and numerous cruisers in the narrows between the Shetlands and Norway, the battleships were able to slip through the blockade on the evening of 26 November, reaching Wilhelmshaven the next day.

Admiral Marschall immediately came under intense criticism from SKL for all aspects of the November raid. Rather than 'rolling up' the cruiser patrol, he had fled from it. His argument that unescorted capital ships had no business engaging enemy light forces at night didn't impress his critics. He was further criticized for failing in the other objective of drawing forces from the South Atlantic by feinting a breakout. That the British cruiser's mistaken report effectively destroyed all hope for that feint succeeding was never seriously considered by his critics. Marschall was allowed to remain as fleet commander but with considerable restriction on his freedom of action. A new level of command, Gruppe West, was inserted between SKL and the fleet commander specifically for the purpose of maintaining tighter shore-based control of the fleet.

While the Kriegsmarine may not have achieved all the success that was possible in the opening months of the war, it came through that period without serious loss or damage. That fortunate situation came to an abrupt end on 13 December 1939 when on two widely separated seas lighter Royal Navy forces inflicted serious damage on much heavier Kriegsmarine units. In the more famous action, the **Admiral Graf Spee,** on her return voyage to Germany, encountered one British heavy cruiser and two light cruisers off the River Plate. The engagement was cleverly managed by the British commander on **Exeter**, Commodore Harwood. He split his forces, sending his two light cruisers **Ajax** and **Achilles** around to **Graf Spee's** other side forcing her commander, Kapitan z. S. Langsdorff, to split his fire. Nevertheless the accuracy of **Graf Spee's** fire soon forced **Exeter** to break off action. Rather than turning to finish off the retreating heavy cruiser, Langsdorff inexplicably turned on the two light cruisers which proved to be much more difficult targets. Some hits were obtained on **Ajax** but the pair stayed with the fight long enough for **Exeter** to effect emergency repairs and rejoin the fray. She was soon again hit and again forced to break off with 94 casualties and only one of nine eight inch guns still able to fire. Again Langsdorff turned against the light cruisers rather than follow the retreating heavy cruiser. He declined to close the two cruisers because of the same fear of torpedoes which had hampered Marschall. There followed a running battle with **Graf Spee** leading **Ajax** and **Achilles** toward the west. At dusk, thinking he had shaken his pursuers when in fact he hadn't (because while they were lost in the increasing dark he was visible against the twilight and the lights of the city), Langsdorff asked and received SKL permission to put into neutral Montevideo, Uruguay for what he considered to be necessary repairs.

The second, less well-known action to occur on 13 December took place as the result of an incredible tactical blunder on the part of SKL. It was a basic naval truism of the day that, in seas where submarine danger existed, small units were used to escort larger ones. Yet for reasons entirely their own SKL decided to send out the light cruisers **Nurnberg, Leipzig** and **Köln** to escort five destroyers through the waters around Heligoland, known to be a favorite hunting ground for Royal Navy subs. The inevitable occurred. The submarine **HMS Salmon** sighted the unescorted light cruisers and put one torpedo into **Nurnberg**, blowing off her bow, and another into **Leipzig** amidships, leaving her dead in the water. Neither ship sank but the damage to **Leipzig** was so severe that she was never again considered truly seaworthy, being relegated to training duties until the desperation of the last days forced her back into action again.

Meanwhile **Admiral Graf Spee** lay in Montevideo as her chances for survival appeared to worsen with each passing hour. Her primary damage had been a single hit in the forecastle which had, in Langsdorff's opinion, impaired her ability to withstand the storms of the North Atlantic and which had at the same time put her fuel and oil filtration system out of action. Considering the distance which **Graf Spee** had sailed since her last refit, this latter damage was serious but it didn't automatically mean that her engines would fail. Once in Montevideo Langsdorff found that international politics was working against him. Rather than the 14 days which he considered necessary for repairs, the Uruguayan government would only grant him three. British propaganda now took its toll. Rumors were spread that strong Royal Navy forces had arrived off the Plate estuary when in fact the only reinforcement had been the replacement of **Exeter** by her sister **Cumberland.** Expecting to face an aircraft carrier and a battlecruiser, Langsdorff chose to land all but a skeleton crew and in the late afternoon of 17 December sailed from Montevideo. With crowds of townspeople lining the shore to see the impending battle **Graf Spee** turned west rather than toward open water, anchored in shallow water and, at dusk, blew herself up. The question of whether Langsdorff was correct in scuttling his ship, saving his crew to attempt a return to Germany, or whether he should have fought what in his mind was a suicidal battle, possibly taking some enemy units down with him, is as much a moral as a tactical question and has no definite answer. The question of whether he should have ever taken his ship into a neutral harbor with damage that was undeniably serious but definitely not crippling is more to the point. Whether he would have been able to lose **Ajax** and **Achilles,** which weren't radar-equipped, whether he would have eluded the converging Allied capital ships, whether **Graf Spee's** engines would have given out because of the damaged filters, whether she would have survived the rough North Atlantic passage back to Germany are unanswerable questions. But it appears that this was where her main chance lay. As soon as Langsdorff decided to turn his ship toward Montevideo, her fate was sealed.

The early winter of 1939-40 proved to be the coldest in a half century. Ports as far south as Boulogne froze solid. Coastal areas of the North Sea and Baltic were particularly hard hit. The unaccustomed ice severely restricted operations of all naval units, particularly lighter forces. Larger units were frequently used to break channels in the ice for smaller ones. Some U-boats were even fitted with temporary 'icebreaker' bows to protect their thin skin. Only in February 1940 did SKL again plan a major naval operation. This was Operation 'Nordmark' set for 18 February, a sortie against the convoy traffic between Norway and England. **Scharnhorst, Gneisenau** and **Admiral Hipper,** accompanied by two destroyers, were to penetrate the Shetland Narrows as far as the latitude of Bergen but ice damage caused the operation to be halted long before any enemy was sighted.

An operation of much more serious consequence occured on the night of 22 February when the 1st Destroyer Flotilla (1. Z-flot. composed of **Leberecht Maass-Z1, Max Schultz-Z3, Richard Beitzen-Z4, Theodor Riedel-Z6, Erich Koellner-Z13** and **Friedrich Eckoldt-Z16)** was sent

On 4 September 1939, the second day of the war, *Admiral Scheer* undergoing major refit at Wilhelmshaven was the object of attack of RAF Blenheim bombers. Two 500 lb. bombs hit but bounced off without exploding. Most of the attacking bombers were lost to German flak. (Bundesarchiv)

...„denn wir fahren gegen Engeland!"

Heute wollen wir ein Liedlein singen:
trinken wollen wir den kühlen Wein
und die Gläser sollen dazu klingen,
denn es muß, es muß geschieden sein.

Unsre Flagge, und die wehet auf dem Maste.
Sie verkündet unsres Reiches Macht;
Denn wir wollen es nicht länger leiden,
daß der Engländmann darüber lacht.

Kommt die Kunde, daß ich bin gefallen,
Daß ich schlafe in der Meeresflut;
Weine nicht um mich, mein Schatz und
denke: Für das Vaterland, da floss sein
Blut.

Gib mir deine Hand, deine weiße Hand,
leb wohl, mein Schatz,
leb wohl, mein Schatz, leb wohl.
Lebe wohl, denn wir fahren, denn wir fahren
denn wir fahren gegen Engeland, Engeland!

If some were dismayed by the opening of hostilities, the official propaganda line was confident. A popular postcard showed *Gneisenau*, with her new 'Atlantic' bow and funnel cap, and carried the lyrics of a patriotic naval song, ". . . denn wir fahren gegen Engeland!" (. . . For we're sailing against England!).

out on Operation 'Wikinger'. The plan was for the destroyers to descend upon the trawler fleet at Dogger Bank at dawn on 23 February. Some of the trawlers were suspected of being Royal Navy auxiliaries, reporting German movements. Any British trawlers were to be boarded and captured. So, loaded with troops for the boarding operations, 1. Z-flot. set out through a swept channel in the coastal minefields on a bright, moon-lit night for a good, old-fashioned pirate raid. Unfortunately two facts which should have urged caution on the operation's planners were either not known or inadequately appreciated. One was the fact that, due to the severity of the winter, the swept channel hadn't been properly cleared in over a month. The other was that on the same evening, the Luftwaffe's X. Fliegerkorps had planned anti-shipping raids on the British coast by the aircraft of KG26. All went well until 1900 hours when fate or coincidence brought all these elements together with disastrous consequences. At that time, while in the midst of Channel 1 of the 'Westwall' barrage, a single He111 of 4./KG26 came upon the destroyers of 1. Z-flot. The pilot of the bomber, being utterly inexperienced in anti-shipping operations, mistook the destroyers for merchantmen. Knowing that no German shipping would be abroad in the North Sea he reasoned that they had to be British and turned to attack. The captains of the destroyers all assumed that the bomber was German but feeling that its actions were decidely aggressive, some ordered their flak crews to send up a few warning shots. Unfortunately the flak rising from below only convinced the bomber pilot that he was dealing with enemy ships. Circling once behind the line of destroyers, he commenced a perfect bomb run, planting three on the trailing ship, **Leberecht Maass**. Thereafter all was confusion. As the remaining destroyers turned to give assistance to **Z1**, the bomber began a second run and claimed two further hits on the same ship. Whether this is indeed what happened is a matter of some controversy. At about the time claimed by the pilot, **Leberecht Maass** did indeed blow up, breaking in two and sinking rapidly. Yet within minutes there was another identical explosion from an unknown source. To further complicate matters a submarine scare then sent the remaining destroyers circling, dropping depth charges at random. Finally, more than 40 minutes after the first attack, the flotilla commander on **Friedrich Eckoldt** realized that all control had been lost and ordered a retreat from the scene. Only then was it realized that a second destroyer, **Max Schultz,** had disappeared, probably the victim of the second, unidentified, massive explosion.

The shock of losing two destroyers to 'friendly' forces was tremendous, especially after 11 mining operations off the English coast had been conducted without damage or loss. The immediate inquiry concluded that the Heinkel had sunk both destroyers. Only when normal minesweeping was resumed again in March was it discovered that a single line of mines had been laid in Channel 1 by British destroyers some time in February. It seems unlikely, but not impossible, that a single bomber armed with five 50kg bombs could sink two 2,200 ton destroyers. What is more likely is that one or both of the massive explosions which sank the two ships were the result of the British mines, not German bombs. The real cause, however, was never identified and corrected: lack of communication between the Luftwaffe and the Kriegsmarine. The staff of X. Fliegerkorps had informed Gruppe West of KG26's operation but Gruppe West never informed the destroyers. And Gruppe West informed the Luftwaffe of 'Wikinger' only after the Heinkel was in the air, too late to influence events. Tragically no common radio frequency existed for air-sea communication. Thus neither the destroyers nor the bomber expected the other to be there and neither could identify itself to the other once contact was made. In the failures of communication at Gruppe West, the Kriegsmarine was paying the price for inserting another level of command between SKL and the fleet. In the failure of communication between the Luftwaffe and the Kriegsmarine, Hitler was paying the price for encouraging rivalry between the branches of his armed forces. Operation 'Wikinger' brought the opening phase of the war to a close on a sour note. Seemingly, what the Royal Navy wasn't able to do to the Kriegsmarine, the Kriegsmarine would do to itself. Of the one heavy cruiser, two light cruisers and two destroyers lost or seriously damaged, German mistakes had been a major contribution in each case. Now political strategy called the sparring of the Kriegsmarine and the Royal Navy in the North Sea to an end. Hitler needed all of his navy for a new adventure: Norway.

The first ships of the Kriegsmarine to go into action against England were the U-boats. What few sea-going boats were available ringed the British Isles on the first day of the war. (Right) The confidence and brash enthusiasm of the young U-boat arm can be seen in the shark-mouth which has been added to the camouflage on the tower of *U25* about to sail for England. (Below) The first victory of the war went to *U30,* seen docking after her first patrol, which sank the liner *Athenia* on 3 September 1939. *U30's* CO, Lemp, mistook *Athenia* for an armed merchant cruiser. (ECPA) (Bottom) The first major warship to be sunk was the aircraft carrier *HMS Courageous* which fell to Schuhart's *U29* on 17 September 1939.

In the first major surface operation of the war, *Gneisenau* (Above) and *Köln* (Left) sortied up to the Norwegian coast on 7 October 1939. The plan was to draw the Royal Navy over a line of U-boats. This plan had failed consistently in the previous war and, not surprisingly, failed again. (NARS, ECPA)

The first naval hero was Kapitänleutnant Gunther Prien, 'the bull of Scapa Flow'. On the evening of 14 October 1939, he took his *U47* into the main British fleet anchorage at Scapa, sank the old battleship *HMS Royal Oak,* and escaped without being detected. On 17 October he brought his boat back to Wilhelmshaven to a hero's welcome and the first Knight's Cross of the war awarded to a sailor. The bull insignia was the invention of Prien's IWO, Engelbert Endrass, who went on to win the Oak Leaves to the Knight's Cross himself. (Bundesarchiv)

The first major loss to the Kriegsmarine came with the scuttling off Montevideo, Uruguay of the heavy cruiser *Admiral Graf Spee*. Encountering three Royal Navy cruisers at the mouth of the River Plate, *Graf Spee* stood off the following attack but damage to her fuel system and low ammunition stocks led her captain to put into Montevideo. (Above & Left) Showing little external evidence of damage, *Graf Spee* was told by local authorities that she could have only three days for repairs. Note the burned out Ar196 float plane, 14 December 1939. (NHC) (Below) Convinced by the British that vastly superior enemy forces awaited him at sea, Langsdorff chose to scuttle rather than fight his ship, 17 December 1939.

In one of the most ill-conceived operations of the war, on 13 December 1939 the light cruisers *Köln, Leipzig,* and *Nurnberg* were sent into the submarine-infested waters off Heligoland to escort home returning destroyers. (Above) The three light cruisers, *Köln* in the foreground, sortie to meet the destroyers. (ECPA) (Below) Not surprisingly, two of the cruisers fell victim to torpedoes from *HMS Salmon*. Here *Leipzig*, her propulsion out, is being towed back to port. She was never again considered fit for front-line duty. (Bundesarchiv)

The most effective element of the North Sea offensive was the destroyer raids to lay magnetic mines off the English coast. Throughout the fall and early winter of 1939-40, 11 raids laid mines which accounted for 76 English ships including three destroyers and six auxiliaries. Not a single German destroyer was lost or seriously damaged. The confidence of the Kriegsmarine in its ability to take on the Royal Navy was tremendously boosted by the apparent ease with which the destroyers were able to conduct the minelaying sorties. The six photos on this and the facing page show the Kriegsmarine's destroyer forces at that time. The attitude of the destroyer men can be seen from the chalked-on-graffiti on the mine cases in the middle photo on the facing page. (ECPA)

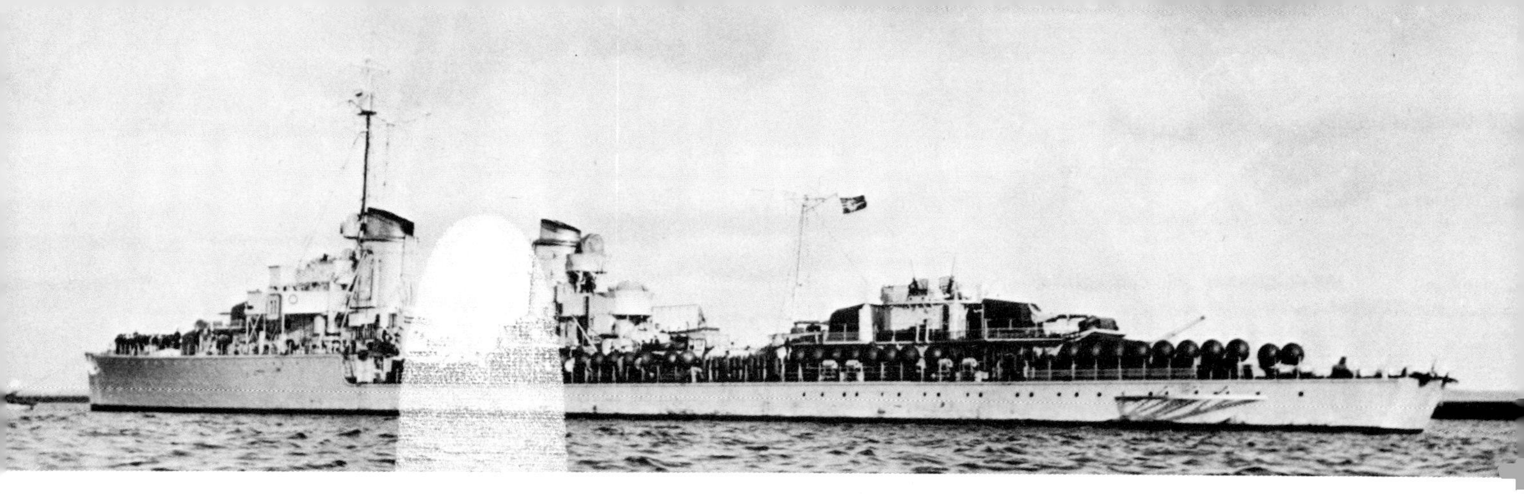

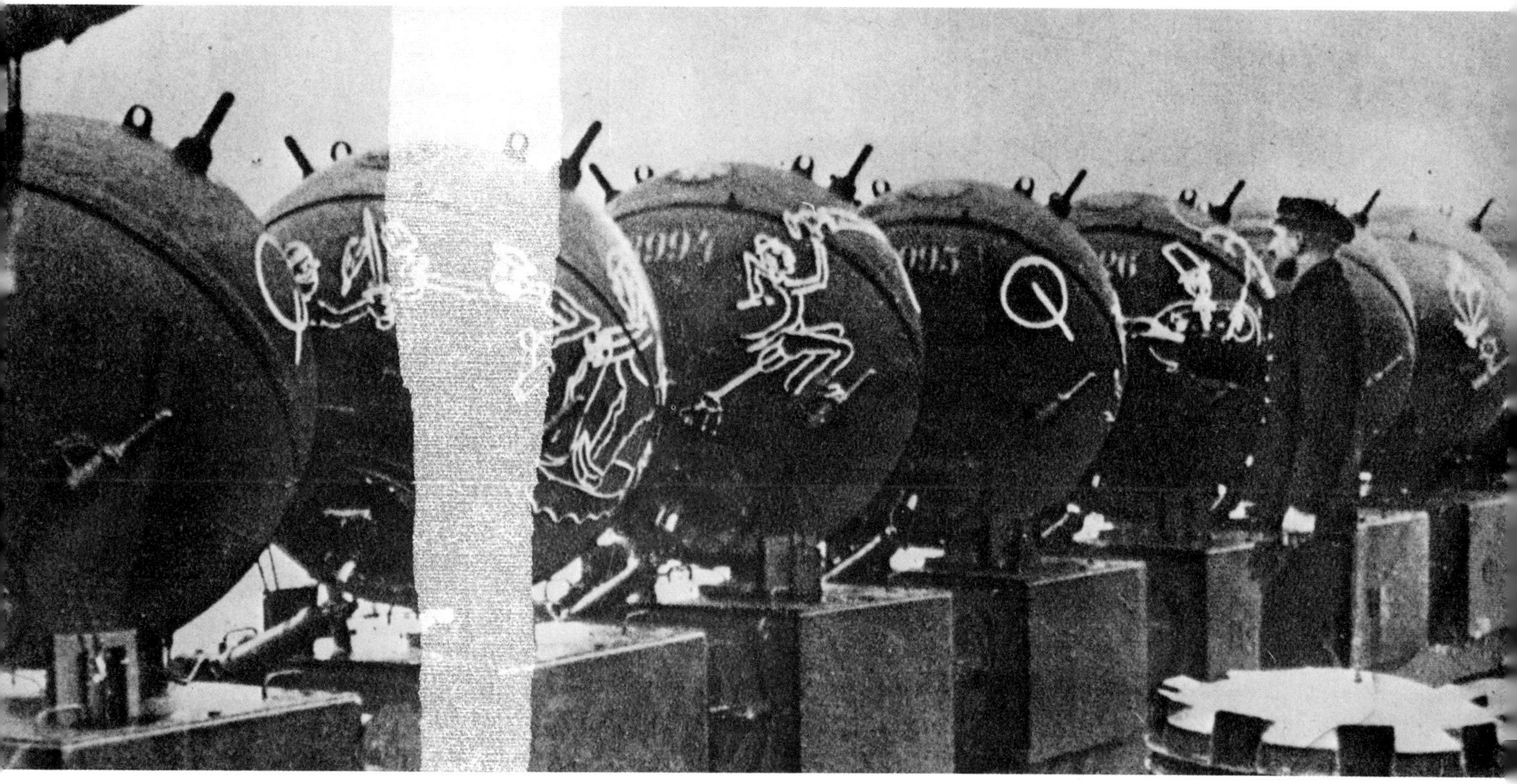

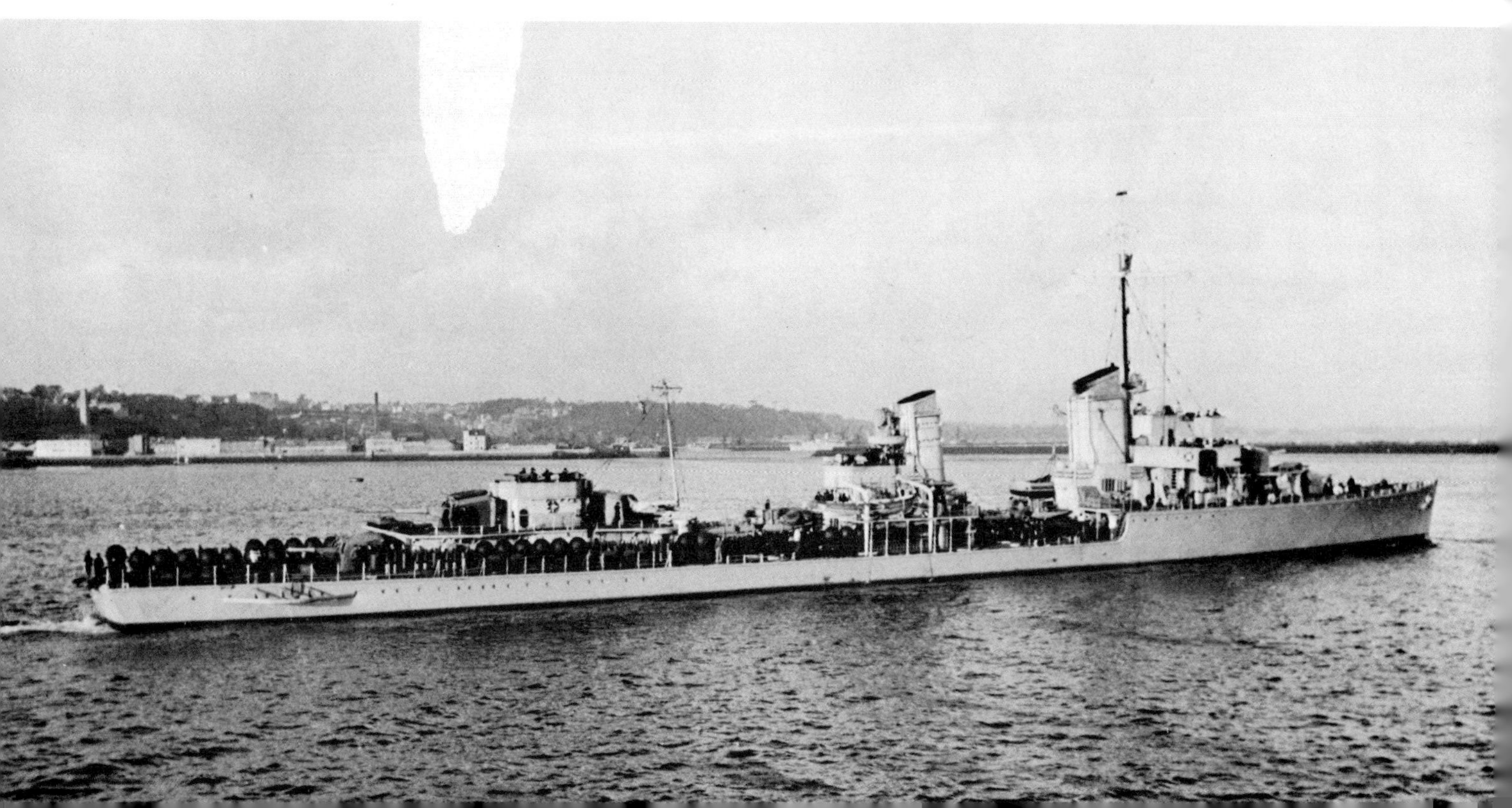

In the midst of the most severe winter in 50 years, SKL decided on Operation 'Nordmark', a sortie by *Scharnhorst*, *Gneisenau* and *Admiral Hipper* into the narrows between the Shetlands and Norway, 18 February 1940. (Above) *Hipper* is seen completely surrounded by ice. (ECPA) (Left) *Scharnhorst* has gotten underway, leaving *Gneisenau* and a destroyer still struggling. (ECPA) (Below) The fleet flagship *Gneisenau* again encounters thick ice. Not surprisingly, ice damage to several of the ships forced cancellation of the sortie. (Bundesarchiv)

Completed in late 1939, *Hipper's* close sister, *Blücher*, is seen working up in the Baltic. She was the first major German warship completed with the 'Atlantic' bow that was retrofitted to most other ships. Her first, and last, operation was 'Weserübung'. (Bundesarchiv)

Weserübung — The Invasion of Norway
April 1940 — August 1940

When the Allies didn't accept Hitler's 'peace' offers after the Polish campaign, planning began for the invasion of France. That campaign was scheduled for May 1940, but another threat increasingly began to insert itself into Hitler's deliberations. Norway came to his attention when, on 5 February, the Allies approved a plan for a mid-March invasion to aid the Finns and again on 16 February when the Royal Navy destroyer **Cossack** chased **Graf Spee's** supply ship, **Altmark**, into a Norwegian fjord to board and sink her. Germany had real reason to fear the fall of neutral Norway to the Allies as most of her iron supplies came from Norwegian mines. For this reason Hitler turned to the Kriegsmarine at the end of February, demanding that it immediately produce plans for the invasion of both Denmark and Norway.

The plan which SKL produced involved virtually every seaworthy vessel that the Kriegsmarine possessed. The warships were to be divided into 12 distinct groups, each with a different mission or troops for a different port. They were:

    Cover Force for Groups 1 & 2: **Scharnhorst & Gneisenau**
    Group 1 (Narvik): **Z2, Z9, Z11, Z12, Z13, Z17, Z18, Z19, Z21 & Z22**
    Group 2 (Trondheim): **Admiral Hipper, Z5, Z6, Z8, & Z16**
    Group 3 (Bergen): **Köln & Königsberg** with 2 TBs & 5 S-boats
    Group 4 (Kristiansand): **Karlsrühe** with 3 TBs & 7 S-boats
    Group 5 (Oslo): **Blücher, Lützow** (ex-**Deutschland**) & **Emden** with 3 TBs & 8 R-boats
plus six smaller groups to Denmark including **Schleswig-Holstein & Schlesien**

The plan was immediately approved by Hitler in spite of some rather dire predictions from SKL about the possible consequences of such a face-to-face confrontation with the Royal Navy. According to SKL the Kriegsmarine could expect to lose half the ships it committed. Seemingly unconcerned about possible losses, Hitler gave the go-ahead at the end of March 1940.

The first ships out of port were seven supply ships that sailed on 3 April, followed four days later by the Cover Group with Groups 1 and 2 which had the farthest to travel. The German moves caught the Royal Navy by surprise. They were themselves in the opening stages of a planned mining of Norwegian coastal waters, Operation 'Wilfred'. When RAF reconnaissance showed the strength of the German forces, the weaker Royal Navy units at sea were withdrawn, but not quite fast enough. At 0910 on 8 April the destroyer **HMS Glowworm** was sighted by **Bernd von Arnim (Z11)**, part of Group 1, which had been trailing behind in a Force 8 gale. **Von Arnim** tried to engage **Glowworm** but found that it couldn't weather the rough seas as well as its British opponent. Responding to **von Arnim's** call for assistance, **Admiral Hipper** turned back. **Hipper** sighted **Glowworm** at 0957 and immediately opened fire. Bursting through **Glowworm's** smoke screen, the two antagonists found themselves only yards apart. Simultaneously both ships turned to ram, the quicker destroyer catching **Hipper** on the starboard bow. The damage to **Hipper** wasn't serious but **Glowworm** was doomed. Caught at pointblank range, she soon capsized and sank under **Hipper's** guns.

During that afternoon Groups 1 and 2 split off from the Cover Group to make toward their intended targets, while the latter took up position off Vestfjord. There **Scharnhorst** and **Gneisenau** encountered the Royal Navy battlecruiser **Renown** and eight destroyers in the midst of patchy snow squalls. In the ensuing engagement, **Renown** was hit twice without serious damage while **Gniesenau** took three hits, one of which knocked out her main battery director control. At this point the Germans felt there could be little gained by further pounding and a great deal to be lost if damaged further. Therefore they used their superior speed to disappear over the northern horizon. The two engagements on 8 April seemed to prove that the doomsayers of SKL had overestimated the threat posed by the British. If the Royal Navy couldn't more effectively intervene, the Germans felt, there was nothing to fear.

On the next morning, 9 April, all invasion groups began their final approaches to their assigned targets. The hope was that the Norwegians would be convinced by the German claim that the occupation was peaceful, being meant only to forestall a similar Allied move. The Norwegians, however, weren't convinced. In spite of the futility of putting up resistance to the overwhelming German might, isolated Norwegian naval units attempted to stop the German advance. At Narvik the old coast defense ships **Eidsvold** and **Norge** were sunk while attempting to stop the destroyers of Group 1. These then landed General Dietl's mountain troops without opposition. Similarly Groups 2, 3 and 4 landed their troops at their respective harbors. Of those Groups only **Köln** suffered any damage, that being sustained in a brief firefight with a shore battery. At Oslofjord, however, Group 5 encountered a nasty surprise. Yet it need never have happened. The most critical part of the 50 mile passage to Oslo was the Drobak Narrows where the fjord was less than half a mile in width and the Norwegians had three forts. All German planning was based on the naive assumption that Group 5 would meet no resistance at Drobak. When the actions of Norwegian patrol boats at the fjord's entrance made it clear that there would be resistance, no one at SKL or in Group 5 paused to consider what would happen at the narrows. The results were predictable. When, at dawn on 9 April, the newly commissioned **Blücher** led the line of German ships into the narrows, she was immediately brought under a heavy and accurate fire from the 28cm and 15cm guns on either side. She was hit repeatedly, her hanger set on fire and her steering jammed at an angle. **Lützow**, immediately behind **Blücher** in line, had her forward turret knocked out, leaving her unable to return fire. To make the tragedy complete **Blücher** then steamed in front of two fixed torpedo tubes at the Kaholm Island fortress. She was hit twice. At 0630 her magazines blew and at 0732 she rolled over and sank. There was nothing for the remaining ships to do but to retreat back down the fjord, landing their troops at Sons-Bukten. Only the next morning, when the troops from Sons secured the surrender of the three Drobak forts, did **Lützow** lead **Emden** into Oslo harbor. The irony is that both SKL and Group 5 had in their possession intelligence reports that described the Drobak forts in precise detail. For leading their warships into obvious danger, in daylight, when the full extent of that danger was known in advance,

Admiral Hipper was assigned to Group 2 of 'Weserübung' to transport part of General Dietl's mountain troops to Trondheim. (Below) *Hipper* lies at Cuxhaven awaiting the arrival of her troops. Her main turret tops have been painted yellow as an air recognition marking in an attempt to avoid a repetition of the disaster of Operation 'Wikinger.' (Bundesarchiv) (Bottom) Inquisitive sailors line the rails as the mountain troops begin to board. (NHC)

the Germans richly deserved the losses they took.

Even with the avoidable loss of **Blücher**, the attrition so far had been much less than expected. This, however, was primarily due to the fact that the German move had caught the British so completely off guard. Now, on 10 April, they began to strike back. The first to be hit was **Königsberg**. She was caught at anchor by two squadrons of Royal Navy Skuas which left her damaged beyond repair. **Karlsruhe**, having dropped her troops at Kristiansand, was on her way back to Germany when she was torpedoed by the submarine **HMS Truant**. When efforts to save her failed, she was finished off by an accompanying torpedo boat. But the British saved their most audacious response for Narvik. Realizing the importance of Narvik to Germany's iron supply, the British made an all-out attempt to deny it to their enemy. Steaming out of the morning mist into Ofotsfjord, the Royal Navy's 2nd Destroyer Flotilla, composed of five H class destroyers, caught ten German counterparts dispersed and off-guard. **Wilhelm Heidkamp (Z21)** was sunk before the Germans even became aware the British had arrived. Seconds later **Anton Schmitt (Z22)** broke in two and followed her sister to the bottom. As the remaining German destroyers reacted, the odds became more even. **Diether von Roeder (Z17)** and **Hans Lüdemann (Z18)** were hit by British shellfire, but **Hunter** and **Hardy** were soon sinking, forcing the British to beat a hasty retreat. On the surface neither side appeared to have won the scuffle. But when the Germans realized that the British had sunk nearly all of the supply ships from which the destroyers were to have rearmed and refueled, the full impact of the 10 April engagement sank in. The eight remaining destroyers at Narvik were effectively immobilized. In spite of their own losses the Royal Navy had succeeded beyond their greatest expectation. Unless the Germans could get supplies to Narvik, the forces there were plums waiting to be picked.

The next few days brought no improvement as the Royal Navy attempted to make up for its failure to interfere with the original invasion. On 11 April, as she was proceeding to Kiel for repair of the damage sustained at Drobak, **Lützow** was torpedoed in the stern by **HMS Spearfish**. Her fantail was almost severed, all steering and propulsion were lost. For several hours it appeared increasingly doubtful that she could be saved as she slowly settled. All excess crew were removed and plans were being made to scuttle her when damage parties finally brought the flooding under control. She was very carefully taken in tow, reaching Kiel the next day. Also on 12 April, **Scharnhorst, Gneisenau** and **Admiral Hipper** made the dash from Trondheim to Wilhelmshaven under the noses of the RAF without suffering any further damage. The latter two immediately went into the dockyard for repair of battle damage. The final chapter of the eight remaining destroyers at Narvik came on 13 April. In the early morning nine Royal Navy destroyers backed up by the battleship **Warspite** steamed into Ofotsfjord to finish the job begun three days earlier. The only effective resistance came from **Georg Thiele (Z2)** which torpedoed **Eskimo** in the bow for damage. One by one the German destroyers were sunk at their berths or trapped in side fjords to be scuttled by their crews. All ten destroyers of Group 1 had ceased to exist.

This last engagement brought 'Weserübung' to a close. After seeming to lead a charmed life for the first two days, many factors – British strength, Norwegian tenacity and German mistakes – all combined to take a serious toll of Kriegsmarine tonnage. While nowhere near the 50% losses predicted, the toll of sunk and damaged ships was still appalling. Starting 'Weserübung' with two battleships, three heavy cruisers, three light cruisers and 14 destroyers, one week later only one battleship (and **Scharnhorst** wasn't really fit because her boilers were again acting up), one light cruiser and four destroyers could be considered ready for further immediate action. Yet, incredibly, 'Weserübung' had succeeded beyond even Hitler's wildest imaginings. With the sole exception of the lives lost when **Blücher** capsized, all troops assigned to Kriegsmarine warships had been safely delivered to their destinations and all targets secured. Only at Narvik was the German conquest of Norway being contested. Narvik harbor was in effective Royal Navy control and Dietl's hold on the town was soon to be contested by advancing Allied troops.

It was Narvik, and the plight of the mountain troops, which led directly to the next German operation and the downfall of Admiral Marschall. By 28 May the Allies had landed enough troops to force Dietl out of the town. With only inadequate aerial drops to keep him supplied, Swedish internment was looking like an increasingly real prospect. A relief force was working its way north from Trondheim but the roads were barely passable in the spring mud. The much quicker sea route was out of the question because the Royal Navy was basing considerable forces at Harstad, northwest of Narvik.

In order to break the English grip on Narvik, SKL quickly worked up a plan for a sortie by the battle squadron, Operation 'Juno'. With **Gneisenau** and **Admiral Hipper** back in service, that squadron was

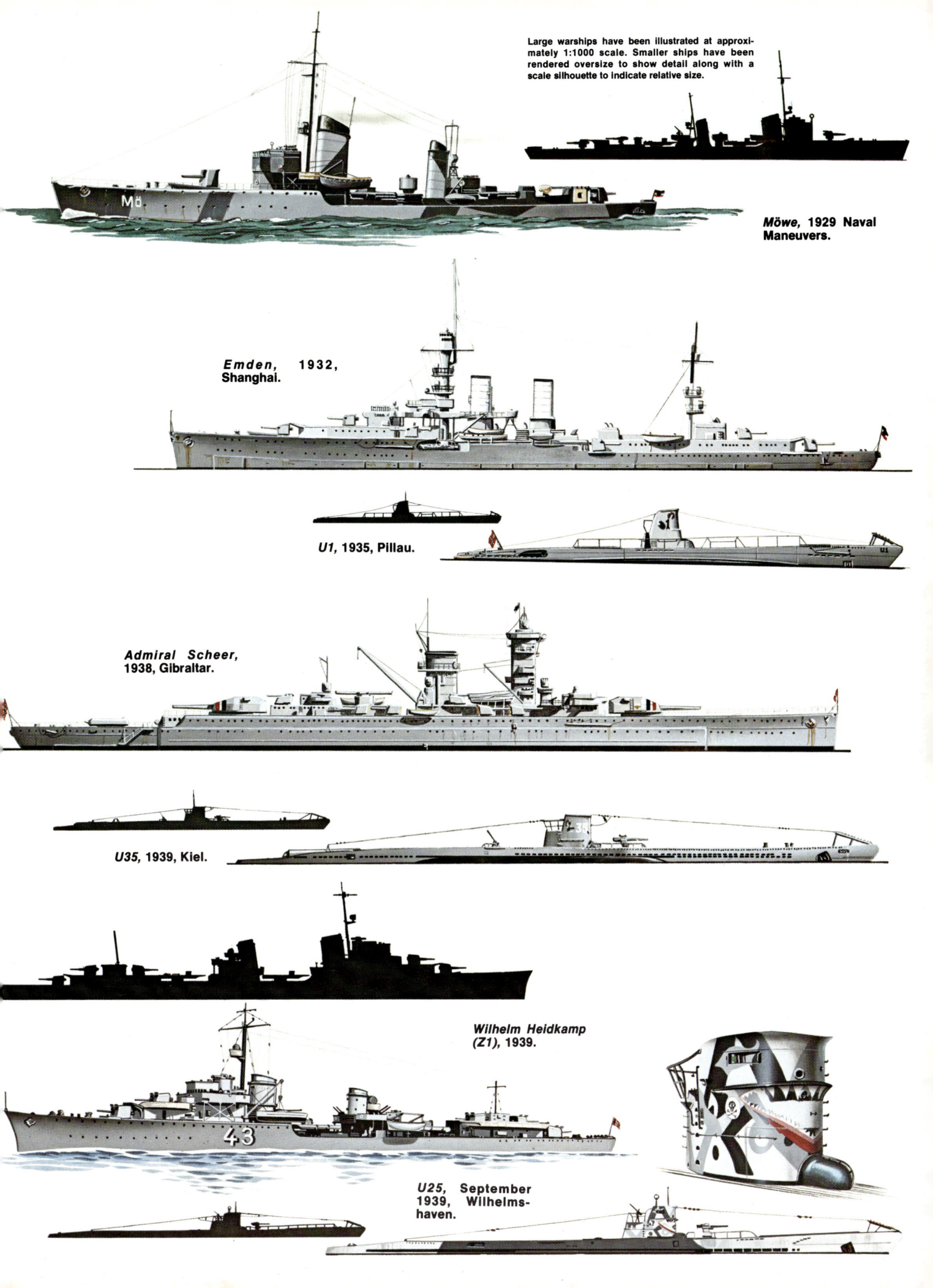

Large warships have been illustrated at approximately 1:1000 scale. Smaller ships have been rendered oversize to show detail along with a scale silhouette to indicate relative size.

Möwe, 1929 Naval Maneuvers.

Emden, 1932, Shanghai.

U1, 1935, Pillau.

Admiral Scheer, 1938, Gibraltar.

U35, 1939, Kiel.

Wilhelm Heidkamp (Z1), 1939.

U25, September 1939, Wilhelmshaven.

back at its strength of six months before. The problem again wasn't one of quality of ships but quality of command. Admiral Marschall, like his predecessor, Admiral Boehm, felt that the fleet commander should have the ultimate decision on tactics within the strategic orders of SKL. Admiral Saalwächter, head of Gruppe West, felt otherwise. Raeder had specifically given him operational control in spite of the fact that he was to remain behind on shore. This conflict over control of the fleet hadn't been adequately resolved when Gruppe West was established in November and remained a festering problem now. To make matters worse, the orders which Marschall was given for 'Juno' were contradictory. He was ordered to penetrate Harstadfjord to attack Royal Navy forces there, to sink targets of opportunity while in transit and at the same time to provide active support for the relief force. Marschall protested to Raeder that there was no way his small fleet could get all those tasks done. He believed he obtained the Grand Admiral's permission to use his best judgement, giving him the freedom of action he desired.

With the command controversy apparently satisfactorily settled, **Scharnhorst, Gneisenau** and **Admiral Hipper**, accompanied by four destroyers, set out from Kiel on 4 June 1940. Unknown to the Germans, on that same day the British decided to withdraw from Narvik because the troops there were needed in France. Three days later, as the fleet refueled off the Norwegian coast, Marschall held a conference of his captains and intelligence staff, correctly deducing from radio traffic that the British were withdrawing from Narvik and that a sortie to Harstad would be pointless. Based on this decision, at dawn on 8 June the fleet began a sweep west of Vestfjord, looking for shipping leaving Narvik. When he informed Gruppe West of his decision, the reaction was furious. Raeder hadn't informed Saalwächter of his conference with Marschall and now Gruppe West, feeling that its authority was being flouted, sent off a series of indignant orders. Saalwächter demanded to know why the fleet wasn't proceeding to Harstad and emphatically ordered it there. While this exchange was proceeding, however, the sweepline encountered four successive English ships. The haul was disappointing. A trawler, a tanker and an empty troopship were dispatched, the hospital ship **Atlantis** was allowed to proceed. After spending the next three hours chasing a phony lead to the southeast, Marschall felt under considerable pressure to produce results. He detached **Hipper** and the destroyers toward Trondheim and the relief force and turned his two battleships again toward the north.

Luck was with the fleet commander. At 1645 **Scharnhorst** and **Gneisenau** came up behind the Royal Navy aircraft carrier **Glorious** and her two escorting destroyers, **Acasta** and **Ardent.** There wasn't much of a fight. Because the wind was behind the Germans, **Glorious** would have had to turn back in order to launch aircraft. Deprived of her primary weapon, she had to trust to her speed to outrun Marschall.

Steaming northward to cover the progress of Groups 1 and 2, *Scharnhorst* and *Gneisenau* provided protection against British interference. All guns are trained out and crews are on alert during the sortie. Note the open rangefinder door on 'Bruno' turret. The two ships did encounter the battlecruiser *HMS Renown* on 9 April 1940 off Vestfjord in a rather half-hearted engagement. (ECPA)

It wasn't enough. By 1721 the Germans had come within range and opened fire. By 1738 **Glorious** had been hit hard. By 1752 she was completely afire and losing way. Her two destroyers turned back in an attempt to cover the damaged carrier, dooming themselves. It was a gallant but futile gesture. By 1815 **Ardent** had been sunk and **Acasta** set on fire. Yet from that sinking destroyer the British managed a small measure of revenge, putting a single torpedo into **Scharnhorst**, bringing her temporarily to a halt. **Gneisenau**, however, was more than enough to finish off **Acasta** and then **Glorious**, which sank at 1900. Feeling relieved that the damage to **Scharnhorst** was a good excuse not to follow Saalwächter's orders, Marschall turned his two ships back to Trondheim, where they arrived the next morning.

Marschall never expected the furious reaction his actions elicited from both Saalwächter and Raeder. The latter claimed he had never given the fleet commander any freedom of action, and both demanded to know why he hadn't proceeded immediately to Harstad. Marschall's defense that he had correctly interpreted British actions, that later aerial reconnaissance had indeed shown that Harstad was empty, that Dietl had reoccupied Narvik on 8 June without any help and that he had engaged and defeated major enemy units impressed neither Admiral. They only saw that their orders had been disobeyed and soon forced Marschall to resign.

This saga of bruised egos and twisted communications was the last main event of the invasion of Norway. Only a few postscripts remained. On 10 June and again on 20 June, **Gneisenau** and **Admiral Hipper** sortied through Trondheim in an attempt to distract the British from **Scharnhorst**. On the second try the submarine **HMS Clyde** put a torpedo into **Gneisenau's** bow. The next day, **Scharnhorst** and four destroyers slipped from Trondheim to Kiel without interference. A month later, on 25 July, **Gneisenau** made a similar dash. On the same day **Admiral Hipper** sailed north on a diversionary raid into the Arctic. The pickings of merchant targets were very thin. She found and sank only one small freighter before returning to Kiel on 9 August, bringing the first Norwegian adventure to a close.

Group 3, the light cruisers *Köln* and *Königsberg*, carried troops to Bergen. (Right) The face of 'Anton' turret, probably on *Köln*, shows more anti-British graffiti. A German sailor is shown poking an umbrella in British Foreign Minister Anthony Eden's eye, saying "Oh, Verzeihung! Oh! Mstr. Eden!! (Oh! Excuse Me! Oh! Mr. Eden!!)" (ECPA) (Below) *Königsberg* as seen from *Köln*, probably on 7 April 1940. Note the yellow turret top in the foreground. (ECPA)

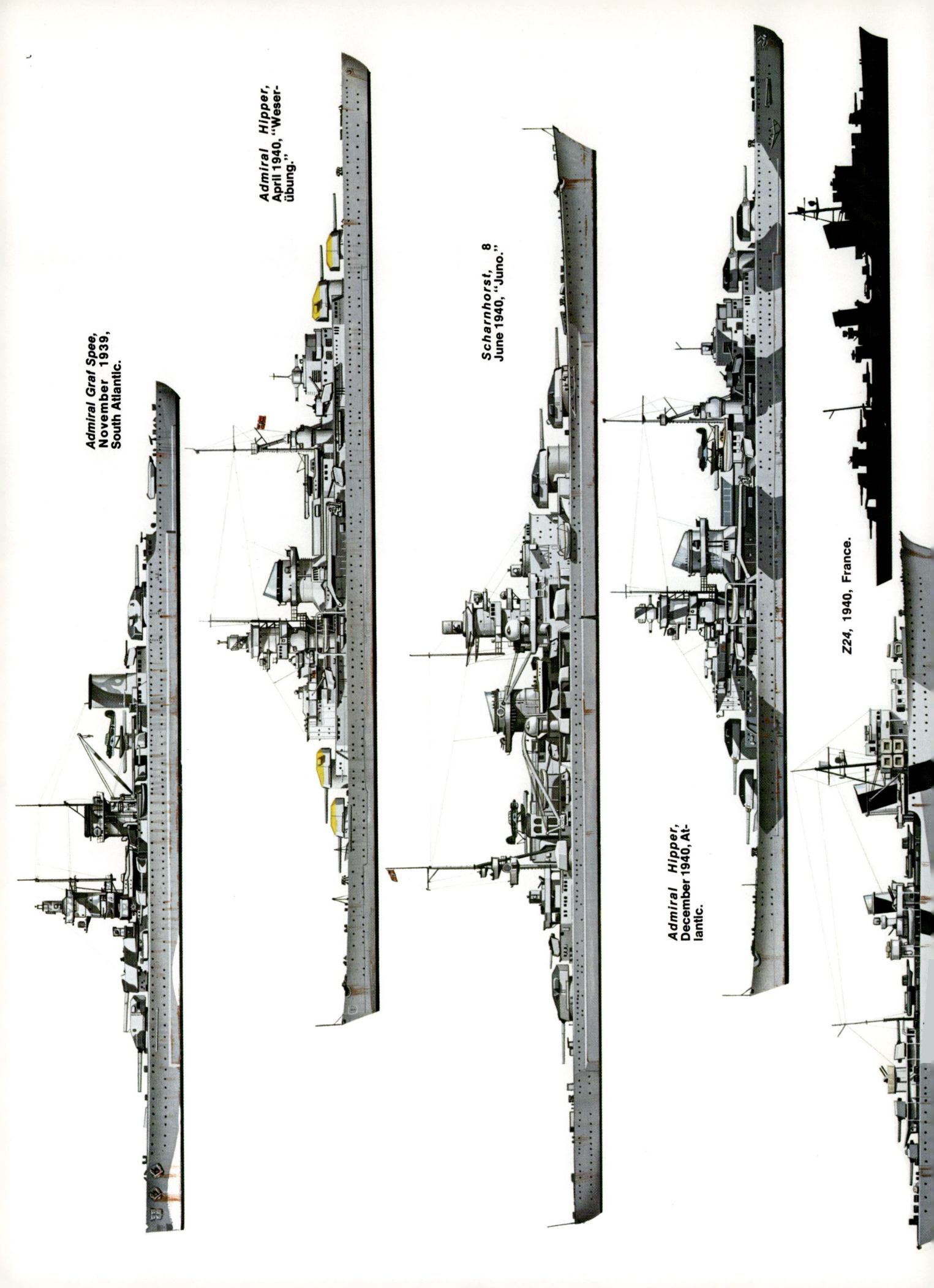

Admiral Graf Spee, November 1939, South Atlantic.

Admiral Hipper, April 1940, "Weserübung."

Scharnhorst, 8 June 1940, "Juno."

Admiral Hipper, December 1940, Atlantic.

Z24, 1940, France.

Nurnberg, Spring 1941, Baltic.

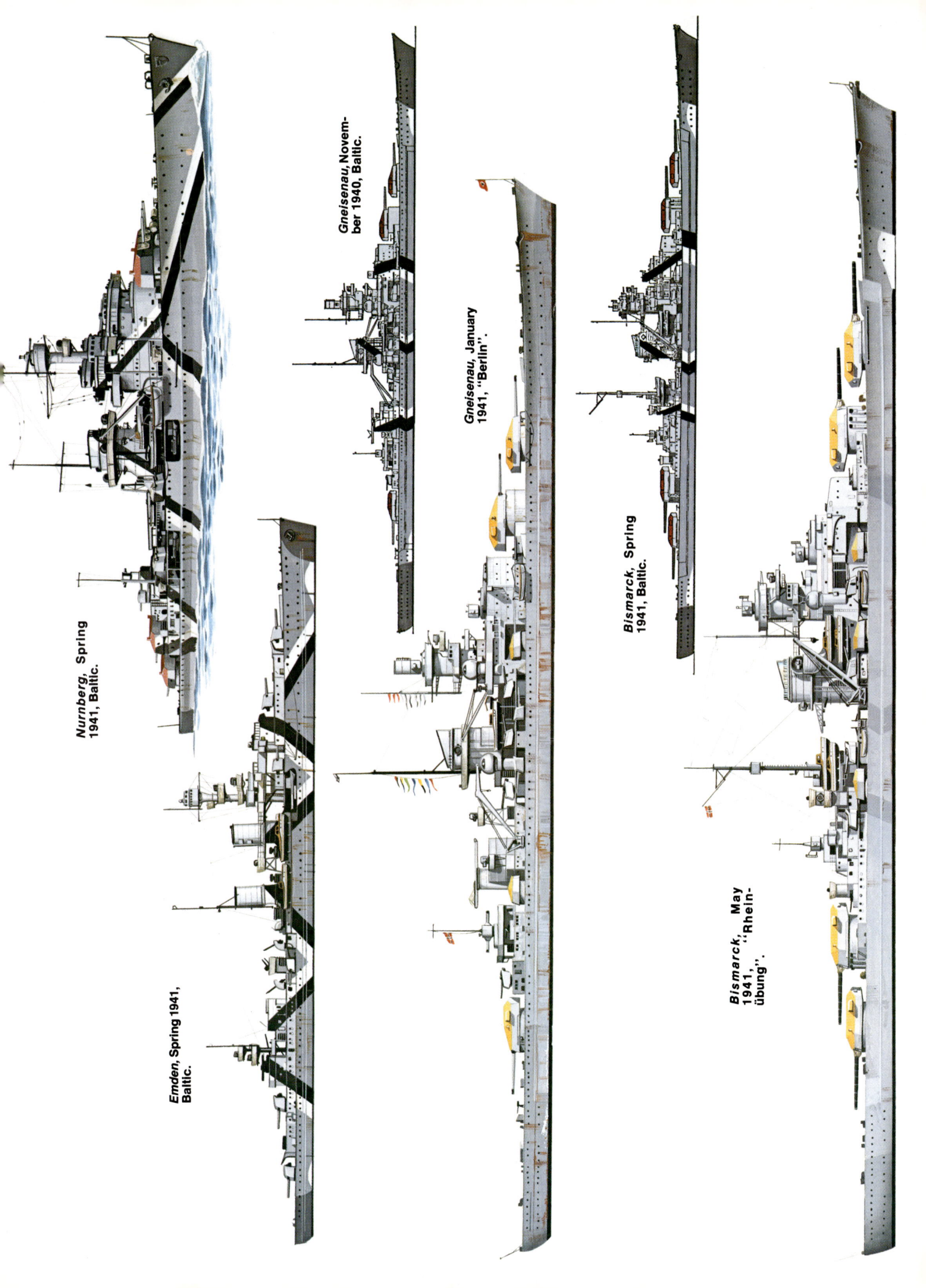

Emden, Spring 1941, Baltic.

Gneisenau, November 1940, Baltic.

Gneisenau, January 1941, "Berlin".

Bismarck, Spring 1941, Baltic.

Bismarck, May 1941, "Rheinübung".

Admiral Hipper saw the first action of 'Weserübung'. (Left) When *Bernd von Arnim* (Z11) of Group 1 encountered a British destroyer on 8 April 1940, *Hipper* turned back to help. *HMS Glowworm* put up valiant resistance, ramming *Hipper* in the port bow, but soon was sunk in the unequal engagement. (NHC) (Below) After the *Glowworm* incident *Hipper* and Group 2 had perhaps the least eventful time of any of the invasion forces. Here one of her four escorting destroyers is seen as they peacefully sail up Trondheimsfjord. (Bundesarchiv) (Bottom) Seen from one of her boats, *Hipper* unloads her troops at Trondheim against no opposition. (NHC)

Other Kriegsmarine forces committed to 'Weserübung' weren't as fortunate in their encounters with the enemy. (Right) *Blücher* ran into a pair of torpedoes at the Drobak Narrows of Oslofjord. She capsized, 9 April 1940. (Below) The Royal Navy also exacted a measure of revenge. A flight of Skuas found *Königsberg* at Bergen and disabled her. (NHC) (Bottom) *Lützow (ex-Deutschland)* was preparing for a second Atlantic sortie when she was diverted to Group 5 of 'Weserübung'. After landing her troops at Oslo, she was returning to Kiel for repairs when *HMS Spearfish* put a torpedo into her stern. For several hours her loss seemed inevitable. Her crew was taken off but she refused to sink and was eventually towed into harbor, 11 April 1940. (Bundesarchiv)

Bremen, 1940, Baltic.

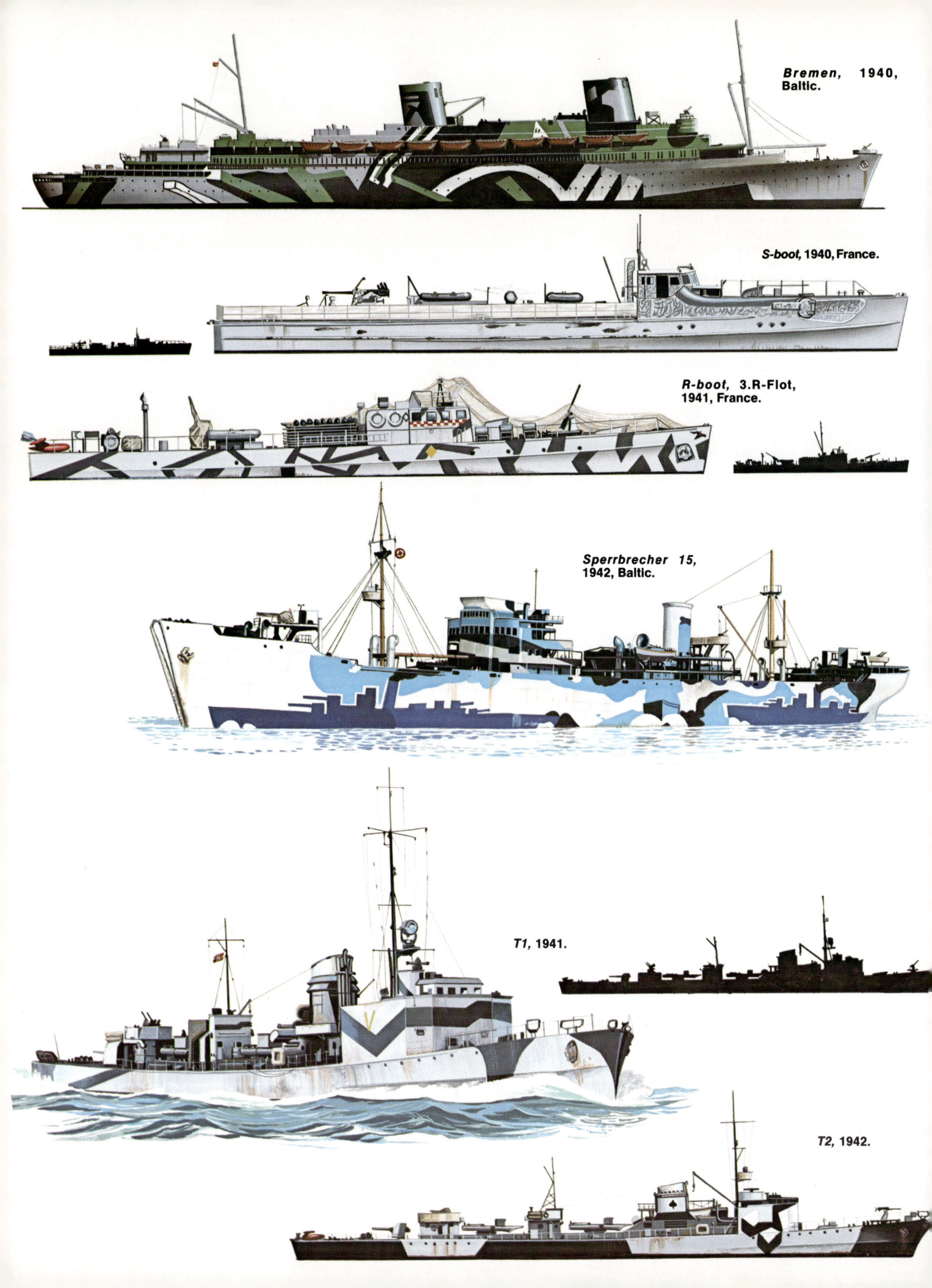

S-boot, 1940, France.

R-boot, 3.R-Flot, 1941, France.

Sperrbrecher 15, 1942, Baltic.

T1, 1941.

T2, 1942.

U3, 1941, ULD-Pillau.

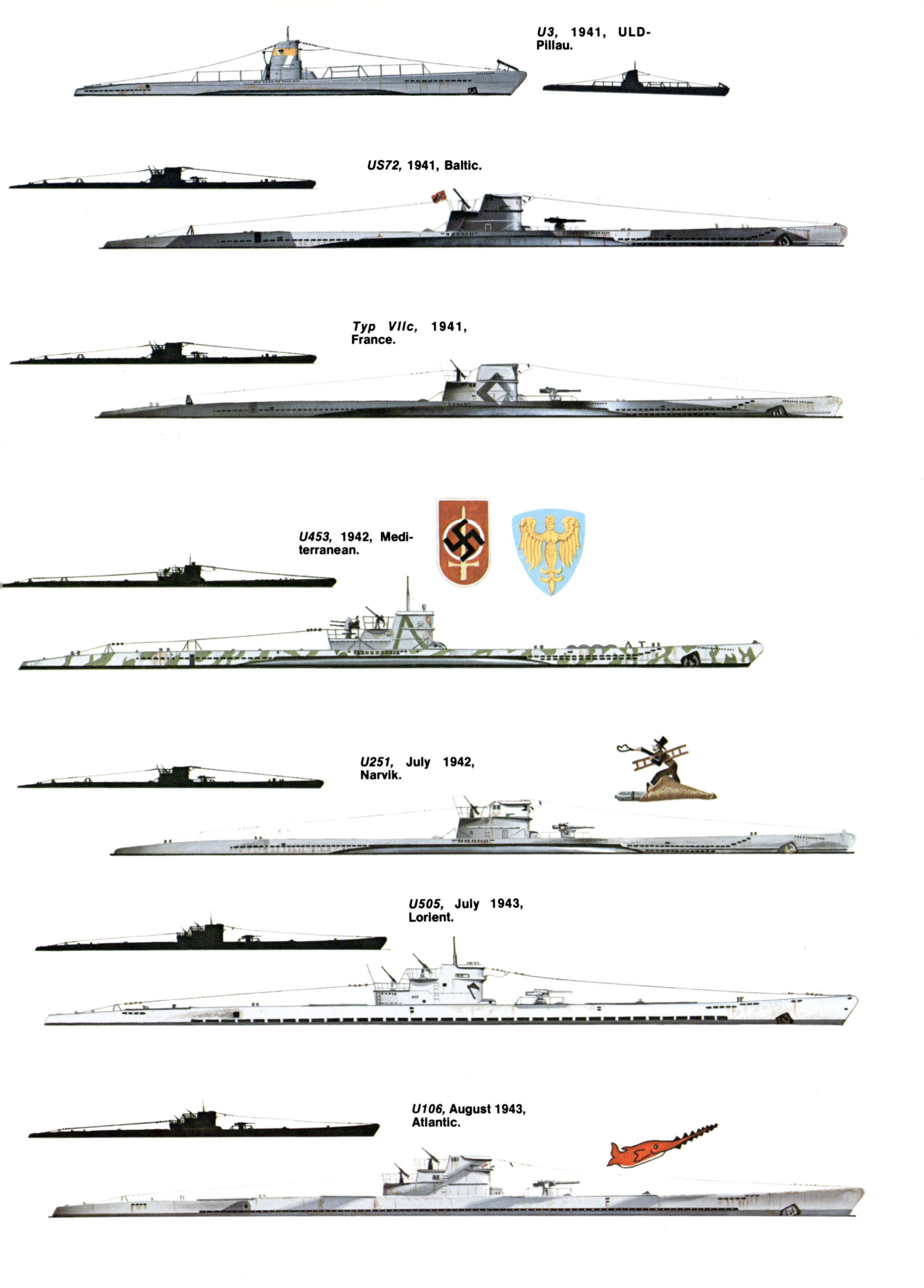

US72, 1941, Baltic.

Typ VIIc, 1941, France.

U453, 1942, Mediterranean.

U251, July 1942, Narvik.

U505, July 1943, Lorient.

U106, August 1943, Atlantic.

Narvik proved to be the grave of Kriegsmarine's magnificent destroyer force. Ten of 22 operational destroyers were assigned to Group 1 of 'Weserübung'. All ten were lost. (Top) All arrived at Narvik safely and disembarked their troops. Here *Hermann Künne (Z19)* lies at anchor off Narvik. (ECPA) (Above) At dawn on 10 April 1940, a force of five British destroyers caught the Germans at Narvik by surprise. *Wilhelm Heidkamp (Z21)* and *Anton Schmitt (Z22)* were sunk and *Diether von Roeder (Z17)* and *Hans Lüdemann (Z18)* were seriously damaged before the remaining Germans came into action. *Diether von Roeder* is seen repairing damage, 11 April 1940 (NARS) (Below) The respite was only temporary. On 13 April 1940 the British finished the job, sinking the eight remaining German destroyers. *Erich Giese (Z12)*, disabled during the battle, was scuttled by her crew. (Ken Macpherson)

The brief interlude following the invasion of Norway allowed the Kriegsmarine to repair quickly those ships which had sustained minor damage. (Above) *Hipper* was immediately drydocked. In order to make her less visible to prowling RAF aircraft, she was painted in a complex multi-color camouflage. This view shows 'Anton' and 'Bruno' turrets. Just visible on 'Anton' is the name 'Glowworm' indicating that this was the turret that finished off that British destroyer. (Bundesarchiv) (Right) This portside view looking forward shows the torpedo control position, an excellent view of a twin 10.5cm mount and the port aircraft handling crane. (Bundesarchiv) (Below) Now out of dock, minus her temporary camouflage and ready to return to action, *Hipper* is seen in the Kieler Förde in the first days of June 1940. (Bundesarchiv)

Scharnhorst, February 1942, "Cerberus".

Emden, 1942, Baltic.

Typ 23 T-boot, February 1942, "Cerberus".

Admiral Hipper, July 1942, "Rösselsprung".

Tirpitz, July 1942, "Rösselsprung".

Lützow, February 1942, Baltic.

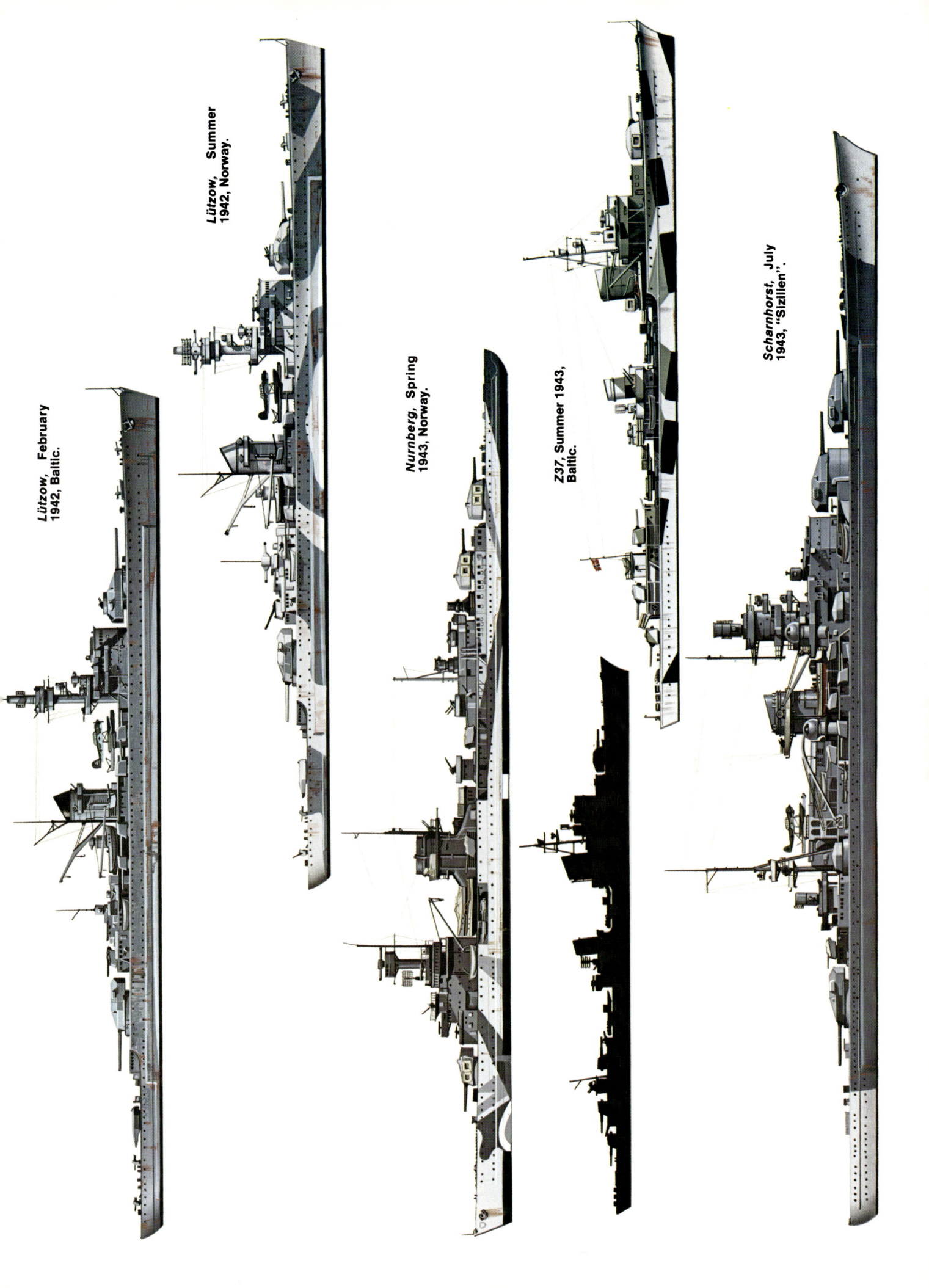

Lützow, Summer 1942, Norway.

Nurnberg, Spring 1943, Norway.

Z37, Summer 1943, Baltic.

Scharnhorst, July 1943, "Sizilien".

The final chapter of 'Weserübung' was Operation 'Juno', a sortie in support of Dietl's beleaguered mountain troops at Narvik. This unique view shows all but two of the ships that took part in 'Juno'. *Gneisenau* is to the left, *Scharnhorst* is directly behind her and *Admiral Hipper* is to the right. Two destroyers and two supply ships are in the background. Note the two He115 float planes and the single He59 sea rescue aircraft. (ECPA)

Beginning on 4 June 1940, Operation 'Juno' was one of the more successful and controversial Kriegsmarine actions, leading directly to the resignation of the fleet commander, Admiral Marschall. (Above) The fleet leaves port for 'Juno', as seen from a trailing destroyer. Leading the line is the oiler *Ditmarschen*, followed by *Gneisenau*, *Scharnhorst*, *Admiral Hipper* and another destroyer. (ECPA) (Right) At 1645 of the same day, *Gneisenau* sighted the prize, *HMS Glorious* and two escorting destroyers. At 1721 she opened fire at the fleeing enemy. Note that the turret tops are dark gray. They were changed from yellow when it was discovered that the British were copying the yellow turret tops in an effort to avoid Luftwaffe attack. After 'Juno', yellow was reinstated as the standard air recognition color. (NHC)

The engagement was a stern chase which *Glorious* had no chance of winning. *Gneisenau*, seen from *Scharnhorst*, had too much speed and firepower. (NHC) (Right) Only when she was burning and already sinking did *Glorious* turn in an attempt to launch aircraft. By then it was too late. Both escorting destroyers were also sunk, but not before *HMS Acasta* was able to put a torpedo into *Scharnhorst*.

Köln, Summer 1943, Baltic.

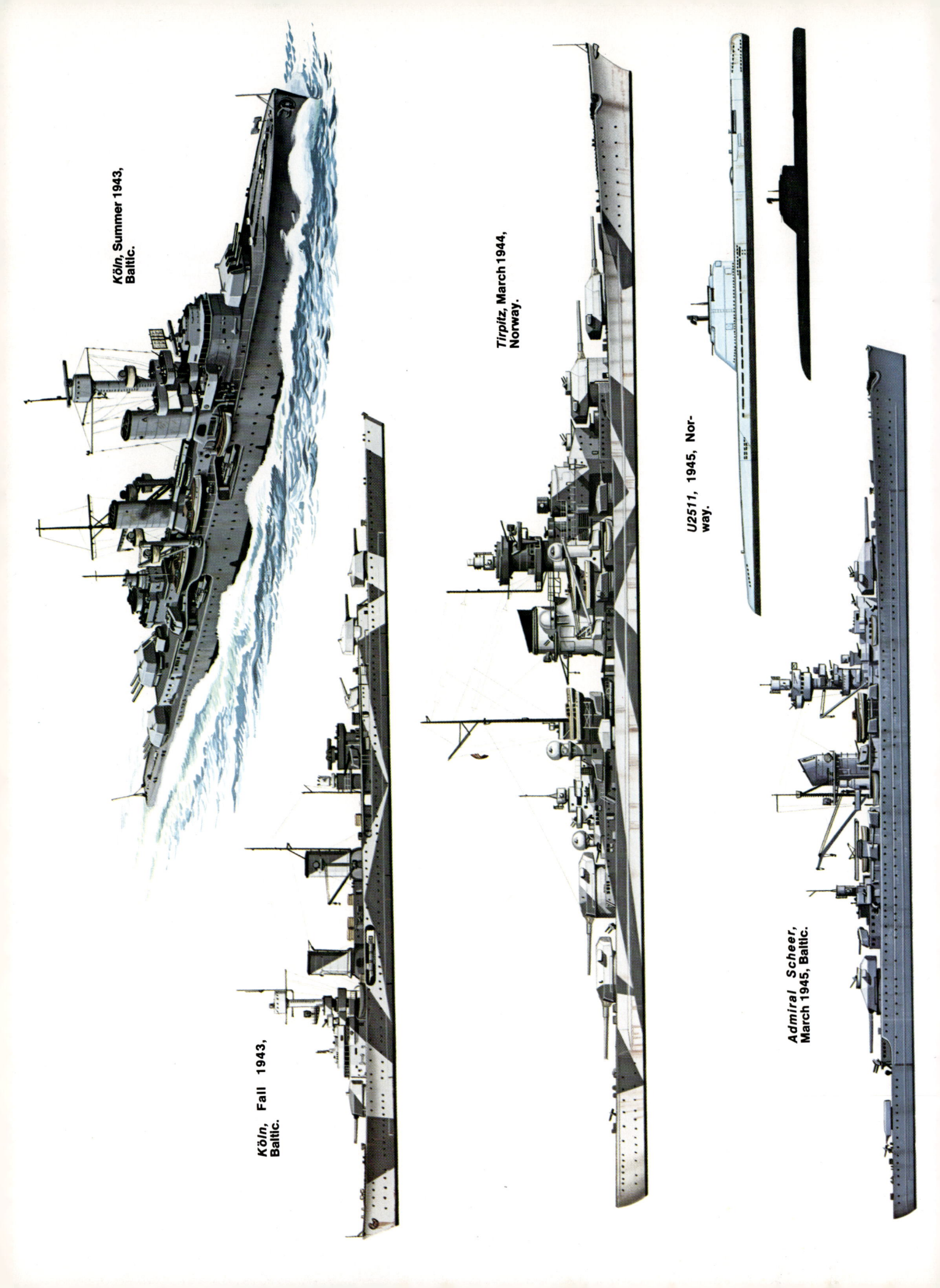

Köln, Fall 1943, Baltic.

Tirpitz, March 1944, Norway.

U2511, 1945, Norway.

Admiral Scheer, March 1945, Baltic.

On 25 July 1940 *Hipper* sortied into the Arctic looking for stray British shipping and hoping to create a diversion for the transfer of *Gneisenau* to Kiel. (Right) *Hipper* leaves Trondheim followed by *Hans Lody (Z10) Friedrich Ihn (Z14)* and *Paul Jacobi (Z5)*. (NARS)

'Weserübung' had cost the Kriegsmarine fewer ships than SKL had feared but still more than it could afford to lose. The most sorely missed, without a doubt, was *Blücher,* so scandalously wasted by poor planning and even worse execution. A memorial on the heights above Drobak Narrows was now all that remained of that once powerful cruiser. (Bundesarchiv)

To the Atlantic,
September 1940 — February 1942

Since the loss of **Graf Spee** in December 1939 no German warship had been at large in the Atlantic. This was in part due more to bad luck than lack of will. SKL had intended to return **Lützow** to the Atlantic in early spring 1940 but first engine trouble, then the planning for 'Weserübung' and then battle damage prevented her sailing. Now that Norway was secure, the vision of SKL returned again to the broad shipping lanes of the Atlantic and the theory and practice of commerce raiding. The only problem they faced was a lack of warships. The only ship immediately available was **Admiral Hipper** and only the capture of the French Atlantic ports had made the use of the relatively short-legged **Hipper** feasible.

The capture of these ports, from Boulogne to Bordeaux, meant a revolution in SKL thinking. No longer could the tragedy of World War I be repeated. No longer could a powerful German Navy be bottled up in the North Sea. No longer could cruiser patrols from Scapa Flow prevent the escape of German raiders. For U-boat command in particular, the acquisition of ports at Brest, Lorient, St-Nazaire and La Rochelle was critical. Now seagoing type VIIs could reach the mid-Atlantic without the long round-trip through the North Sea. With in-transit time cut in half, Dönitz had his fleet effectively doubled without adding a single boat. For the surface fleet only two ports had the proper facilities. Le Havre was the best equipped but was just too close to England. Only St-Nazaire and Brest had adequate facilities and location and the latter port, located at the tip of the Breton peninsula, was the obvious first choice. The vision of a fleet of surface raiders operating from Brest, with the wide Atlantic at the doorstep, couldn't help but entice the planners of SKL.

With all this in mind, **Admiral Hipper** was prepared for an Atlantic sortie as soon as she returned from the Arctic. She left Kiel on 24 September 1940 but this raid wasn't to be. Off Stavenger she developed engine trouble, the curse of German capital ships, and by 30 September was back at Kiel for repairs. SKL was in an embarrassing situation. The Atlantic beckoned and there wasn't a single major ship available for operations.

This situation didn't change until mid-October when the heavy cruiser **Admiral Scheer**, having completed a year-long rebuild, was declared ready for service. Leaving Wilhelmshaven on 27 October **Scheer** reached the Atlantic traffic lanes without being detected. After a week of fruitless patrolling, she stumbled onto convoy HX84 (37 ships) on the afternoon of 5 November. After quickly sinking a straggling steamer, **Scheer** was engaged by the armed merchant cruiser **HMS Jervis Bay**. The British ship was gallant but totally out-classed, sinking at 1700, 20 minutes after the engagement began. Before the engagement began, the convoy commander had ordered the ships to scatter. Now **Scheer** set out to sink as many as she could find. Before dark, five of the scattered merchantmen had been sunk and three more damaged. The British reaction was immediate. The next two HX convoys were recalled. Two battleships and three battlecruisers were deployed across her possible return routes, but **Scheer** turned to disappear into the South Atlantic. A 'lost' raider at large was every bit as effective in disrupting shipping traffic as one astride the shipping lanes.

A second worry was added when **Admiral Hipper** succeeded in her next attempt at the Denmark Straits on 6 December. After almost three weeks of searching, she too encountered a prize, a southbound troop convoy WS5A (20 ships), off the coast of Spain. The convoy was well guarded by three heavy cruisers and two aircraft carriers loaded with planes for the Mid-East. **Hipper** engaged the cruiser **HMS Berwick** before she realized the total strength of the escort. **Berwick** was quickly hit twice but **Hipper's** captain, Kapitan z. S. Meisel, saw he was getting into more than he bargained for and quickly disengaged. **Hipper** did manage to damage two of the convoy's ships and on her way to Brest she caught and sank a small steamer. On 27 December 1940, with her engines again acting up, **Admiral Hipper** became the first major German warship to dock at one of the French ports.

The very next day SKL tried its most ambitious Atlantic raid yet. **Scharnhorst** and **Gneisenau**, in service again after their Norwegian actions, were to be sent on Operation 'Berlin'. The plan would have again doubled the number of German ships in the Atlantic but **Gneisenau** suffered storm damage to her newly repaired bow and both ships were back at Kiel on 2 January 1941. On 22 January 'Berlin' was attempted again. By 28 January the two were south of Iceland where they were intercepted by a pair of light cruisers of the Northern Patrol. The new fleet commander, Admiral Gunter Lütjens, had no intention of following his predecessors in their dispute with SKL or Gruppe West. His orders were to avoid engagement with enemy naval units so as not to risk damage that might slow down his ships. Accordingly Lütjens turned and retreated to the north. On the evening of 3 February, he tried again, this time passing the Denmark Straits unobserved. On 8 February convoy HX106 was sighted but Lütjens chose not to attack when the old battleship **HMS Ramilles** was identified in the escort. No further targets were sighted until 22 February when five independent steamers from a dispersed convoy were caught and sunk. Turning south, looking for more victims, the two battleships headed for the Canary Islands. On 7 March convoy SL67 was sighted but again not engaged because of the presence of another old battleship, **HMS Malaya**. Turning northward again, Lütjens found the ideal target, an unescorted convoy. On 15 and 16 March, the two battleships had field days, **Scharnhorst** sank six ships of 35,000 GRT while **Gneisenau** sank seven of 26,600 GRT and captured three tankers of 20,000 GRT. While engaged in picking up the survivors from her last victim, **Gneisenau** saw the Royal Navy battleship **Rodney** approaching at high speed but was able to work up to speed under a smoke screen and avoid the slower British ship. On 23 March the two German battleships put into Brest, having completed a highly successful cruise.

While **Scharnhorst** and **Gneisenau** had been so rewardingly engaged, **Admiral Hipper** again sortied. Leaving Brest on 11 February, she met with immediate success. On that same day she met and sank a straggler from convoy HG53. The next day she came upon the nine ships of the unescorted convoy SLS64, sinking seven. By 15 February she was again back at Brest. For that brief four day period in February 1941 the commerce raiding strength of the Kriegsmarine reached a peak. Never again would four major German ships be at large on the oceans of the world.

On 15 March **Admiral Hipper** again left Brest, this time on her way back home for a long overdue refit. On 23 March she passed unnoticed through the Denmark Straits, arriving at Kiel five days later. Following on **Hipper's** heels, **Admiral Scheer** passed through the straits on 26 March, reaching Bergen four days later and Kiel on 1 April 1941.

The great raids were over. **Scharnhorst** and **Gneisenau** were at Brest, **Admiral Hipper** and **Admiral Scheer** were at Kiel. The results had indeed been spectacular. Operation 'Berlin' had netted 22 ships of 115,600GRT, **Scheer** had sunk 17 of 113,300GRT and **Hipper** sank nine of 38,800GRT. U-boat commander Dönitz argued that the results ceased to be as impressive when the effort involved was considered. During the same period in which these raids occurred, Dönitz' U-boats sank twice as much tonnage while never having more than 15 boats at sea at any one time and while employing less than a quarter of the over 6000 men that made up the crews of the four big ships (and without having to flee from enemy battleships). But equally as important as the tonnage sunk was the immense propaganda value of the raids. Having 'ruled the waves' for centuries, the fact that four enemy warships could roam the oceans seemingly at will was a tremendous blow to the Royal Navy's pride and prestige. It was a blow that the Royal Navy felt very deeply, resolving never to let it happen again. The Kriegsmarine would be made to pay.

Part of the price the British intended to exact was the immobilizing of the two battleships lying at Brest. While the combination of location and facilities at Brest made it ideal, SKL had neglected one very important fact. Brest was less than half the distance from England than was Wilhelmshaven, which the RAF had raided on the second day of the war. Within two weeks of their arrival at Brest, **Gneisenau** had again been holed by a torpedo. On 10 April she was hit again, this time by four bombs, indefinitely postponing plans for a second Atlantic sortie.

While the British had their attention held in the Atlantic, important events were taking place in the Baltic. Three major new warships were working up to operational readiness. The heavy cruiser **Prinz Eugen** (an improved half-sister to **Admiral Hipper**), and the battleship **Bismarck** were ready for action. **Bismarck's** sister, **Tirpitz**, was two months into her six month training period. These two were 'real' battleships (the Royal Navy had always considered **Scharnhorst** and **Gneisenau** to be battlecruisers because of their 28cm main armament). Armed with eight 38cm (15″) guns in four turrets and strongly armored, they were still fast enough to outrun nearly all British capital ships. Individually they were strong. Operating as a team they would have been able to take on any convoy, even if protected by a battleship. Yet they were fated never to operate together. SKL was eager to use the two ships that were available. With **Hipper** and **Scheer** in dock and **Scharnhorst** and **Gneisenau** immobilized at Brest, the Kriegsmarine was again without ships with which to raid. They were unwilling to wait the four months for **Tirpitz**' training to be completed and equally unwilling to shorten that training. Therefore, SKL decided on a new operation, 'Rheinübung'. **Bismarck** and **Prinz Eugen** were headed for the Atlantic.

'Rheinübung' was originally planned for late April but had to be delayed when **Prinz Eugen** suffered minor mine damage. Only on 18 May did the two ships leave Gotenhafen for their dramatic sortie. If they were successful, they could make further Atlantic missions easier for any ship that followed. The British were determined that they should fail. At virtually every step along the route they were observed by British agents or aircraft. On 21 May they stopped at Korsfjord near Bergen to allow **Prinz Eugen** to refuel. Admiral Lütjens on **Bismarck** decided not to top off his own ship's tanks. Early the next morning the two sailed, entering the Denmark Straits on the evening of 23 May. There they met the inevitable cruisers of the Northern Patrol. The heavy cruisers **Norfolk** and **Suffolk** exchanged a few long-range shots with the Germans, then settled down to trailing them through the snowy night, tracking them by radar. When the cruisers kept on reappearing on their trail after long periods of low visibility and evasive maneuvers, the realization came to Lütjens that the British ships were radar-equipped. It was quite a shock. Kriegsmarine ships had had sea-borne radar since 1938 but it wasn't particularly reliable or efficient. Naval intelligence had confidently assured SKL that the British had no similar device. Thus the discovery that the trailing cruisers had radar at least as good as his own caused Lütjens considerable dismay. This may explain some of his uncharacteristic behavior of the next day.

As the sun rose on 24 May 1941, Lütjens found he had more to deal with than two heavy cruisers. Out of the east came the shapes of two enemy capital ships, steaming straight at him at high speed. In the past, whenever Lütjens had encountered large enemy ships, he had always disengaged. He was, after all, under standing orders not to endanger his ships. But now he apparently felt himself trapped, committed to an engagement which his instincts and orders told him to avoid. With ice to the west, unidentified capital ships to the east and radar carrying cruisers behind him, his options did indeed appear limited.

The British capital ships, which proved to be the battlecruiser **Hood** and the brand-new battleship **Prince of Wales,** opened the engagement at 0553. In order to shorten the range so that **Prince of Wales'** 14″ guns could be effective, the two British ships continued on a closing course for several minutes after opening fire. This proved to be a mistake because it allowed the German ships to fire full salvoes while limiting the British to their forward turrets. The German fire, normally accurate, was unusually so on this occasion. Within three minutes **Prinz Eugen** obtained hits on **Hood,** setting her hanger on fire. At 0600, with the range down to 15km, disaster struck. Admiral Holland on **Hood** ordered his ships onto a parallel course in order to finally bring all guns to bear. At that same instant **Hood** was straddled by a full salvo of 38cm shells from **Bismarck**. At least one shell from that salvo hit **Hood** aft, penetrating to her after 15″ magazine. She blew up, the after part of the ship coming completely apart, the forward part slipping under the waves in less than a minute. Of her complement of 1419 officers and men there were only three survivors.

Understandably the reaction on **Prince of Wales** was shock. On the German ships there was jubilation. Neither side, however, took time to contemplate the disaster. By 0602 **Prince of Wales** was under a heavy and accurate fire from both German ships which she was able to return only fitfully. Between the enemy fire and mechanical breakdowns in her new turrets soon only two of her ten 14″ guns were operable. Wisely Captain Leach disengaged at 0613, turning away from the Germans. They didn't pursue.

Aboard the German ships there was great joy. For the first time in 25 years German and British battleships had stood off and slugged it out with each other. The results had been spectacular, **Hood** had blown apart and **Prince of Wales** had fled. (A few of the more historically minded Germans may have been sobered by the fact that it was **Hood** which had blown apart. British battlecruisers had shown a tendency to do that since three were lost to magazine explosions in one afternoon at Jutland.) German fire had repeatedly hit the British ships while only three hits had been obtained by the British, all by **Prince of Wales** on **Bismarck.** Yet within a few minutes the realization sank in that the victory hadn't improved Lütjens' position in the least. In fact it was quite a bit worse. **Prince of Wales** had fled but not far. She now joined the two trailing cruisers, continuing to shadow at a safe distance. But worse was the fact that one of the three 14″ hits on **Bismarck** had been a lucky shot that penetrated her bow at the waterline, piercing one of her main oil tanks. This caused a serious oil leak, reducing her fuel supply and creating a continuous oil slick that would make losing her pursuit even more difficult.

For the remainder of that day **Bismarck** led **Prince of Wales** on a high-speed southward chase. The British were content to remain out of range, having no desire to re-engage the two Germans until reinforcements arrived. They knew that every minute brought other Royal Navy units closer. Every effort of the Germans to shake the pursuit failed. Finally at 2000, as day gave way to the long Arctic twilight, **Bismarck** slowed down, bringing **Prince of Wales** under fire. The intent of this maneuver was to distract the British from the fact that **Prinz Eugen** was slipping away to the southwest. Having had a long day to contemplate his situation, Lütjens had decided that **Bismarck's** fuel situation

During 1940 in accordance with the Russo-German Non-Aggression pact, Germany bought large quantities of Russian oil and wheat. Part of the return payment was the recently launched hull of the fourth 20cm cruiser, which was to have been named *Lützow*. She is seen here being towed off to Kronstadt, where she was renamed *Petropavlovsk* and later *Tallin*. She was never fully operational in the Soviet Navy but was used extensively as mobile artillery against the Germans (Bundesarchiv)

The new ships which the Kriegsmarine hoped would give them the power to challenge the Royal Navy began to be completed in the fall of 1940. *Prinz Eugen,* a close half-sister to *Hipper,* was commissioned at Kiel on 1 August 1940. (NARS)

wouldn't allow her to proceed on her commerce raiding mission. He therefore decided to release **Prinz Eugen** to continue the operation while **Bismarck** turned southeast toward Brest. The ploy worked. When the ships settled again on a southward course, only one ship led the parade.

Just before midnight help arrived for **Prince of Wales** in the form of the aircraft carrier **Victorious.** A raid by nine torpedo planes was launched. All nine found **Bismarck** and one hit was obtained but that exploded harmlessly against her waterline belt. Benefitting from the confusion of the raid, **Bismarck** now altered her course to the southeast. Neither the British lookouts nor their radar caught this maneuver and soon **Bismarck** had been lost. When the next morning showed **Bismarck** a clear horizon, Lütjens still assumed he was being tracked by the British. The shock of discovering that the British carried radar which appeared to be far superior to the German ruled his thinking. Acting as if his position were known, Lütjens kept up a sustained radio traffic with SKL, supplying the British invaluable clues as to his whereabouts. They had assumed that Bismarck had continued southward. All pursuit had been based on this assumption. But the position indicated by HF/DF (High Frequency/Direction Finding) of her radio traffic told the British for the first time that she was bearing eastward toward Brest. The Royal Navy reacted to this new information by bringing up Force H (**Ark Royal** and **Renown**) from Gibraltar and redirecting the battleships **King George V** and **Rodney** from convoy duties. Yet, while the British may have now been told the direction in which **Bismarck** was moving, they still didn't know her exact location. Throughout 25 May she remained lost to them, only being rediscovered by an RAF Catalina which spotted her oil slick on the morning of 26 May.

She was rapidly getting closer to the French coast. Knowing that by the afternoon of 26 May she would come under the protection of shore-based aircraft, the converging British went to full speed in a desperate attempt to catch the fleeing battleship. At noon she was sighted by a patrol plane from **Ark Royal.** Immediately a raid was launched. When that raid misfired, the British cruiser **Sheffield** being attacked by accident, a final attempt was made in rapidly deteriorating weather. This wave succeeded in finding **Bismarck.** 15 obsolete Swordfish torpedo planes came in on a totally uncoordinated attack on the battleship. Against all odds two hits were obtained. One proved critical. A torpedo hit right aft in her steering compartment jammed her rudder hard over, rendering her nearly unmaneuverable.

Her fate was sealed by that single torpedo. Only by using her opposite side engines could she keep on anything resembling a proper course. The freshening gale kept forcing her off course, toward the onrushing **Rodney** and **King George V.** That night the Royal Navy's 4th Destroyer Flotilla found her, taking up positions on all sides of her so that she would not again give them the slip. In her present condition, however, that wasn't very likely. At dawn on 27 May she came under fire from the guns of the two British battleships, who pounded her into submission. She was eventually finished off by torpedoes from the cruisers **Dorsetshire** and **Norfolk,** finally sinking at 1035.

The answers to numerous questions followed Lütjens to his death. Why he continued to press southward after being sighted by the British cruisers is perhaps the most obvious. During Operation 'Berlin' in January he had turned back after being sighted by patrol cruisers and had been able to break into the ocean unobserved a few days later. This time, however, he pressed on. The most likely answer is that he felt confident that he could shake his pursuit in the intermittent snow squalls that night. Whether that indeed was his thinking will never be known but whatever reason caused him to continue, sealed **Bismarck's** fate. Again why, when he had discovered the British radar, did he not then attack the cruisers is another unanswered question. As long as his movements were known to the British, he must have been aware that every moment brought other Royal Navy ships closer. A third question was why, after **Hood** had been sunk and **Prince of Wales** forced to flee he didn't then turn on his pursuit. There is every reason to believe that he could have finished off the British or at least forced them to break contact. Most likely he didn't attack in either case because of his standing orders. He could fight to defend himself, as he did when **Hood** and **Prince of Wales** closed, but he couldn't take needless risks and attack. He apparently refused to the end to violate his orders. He had no intention of being the third fleet commander relieved for unwillingness to follow orders. It was the trap of this blind obedience and the 'psychological trap' caused by the discovery of the British radar which led to **Bismarck's** early loss, which wouldn't allow Lütjens to follow options which might have changed the story.

The sad postscript to 'Rheinübung' was played out by **Prinz Eugen.** Having broken away from **Bismarck** at dusk on 24 May, she had set off to raid on her own among the shipping lanes. But the engine troubles which plagued **Hipper** struck her too and by 29 May she was in Brest for major engine repairs. She hadn't sunk a single enemy ship.

The outcome of the 'Rheinübung' was a disaster for the Kriegsmarine. Hitler had felt a particular attachment to **Bismarck.** She was, after all, the first German battleship in 23 years and the pride of the nation. When informed of her victory over **Hood,** Hitler had been euphoric. When informed of her loss he was enraged, demanding an inquiry into the SKL plans that had sent her to her fate. While Hitler's probe into the 'Atlantic Strategy' was in progress, other events occurred which did nothing to

(Above) *Bismarck* was commissioned on 24 August 1940. As with *Prinz Eugen*, *Bismarck* now faced a rigorous six month training period before she would be ready for service. (Bundesarchiv) (Below) *Bismarck* is seen soon thereafter, as she began her working up. Note that she is still lacking her main rangefinder. (NHC)

strengthen the Kriegsmarine's position. On 13 June **Lützow,** which had been out of service for a year following 'Weserübung', was sighted and torpedoed by RAF Beauforts while attempting a breakout into the Atlantic. The damage was extensive with half of her power plant out of action and a heavy list. She limped back to Kiel where she would be until January 1942. On 1 July **Prinz Eugen** was hit by a single bomb forward while at dock in Brest. The hit was a serious one. It destroyed the below-decks control center that directed her main battery fire. On 23 July **Scharnhorst's** engine overhaul was completed and she was moved to La Pallice in an attempt to escape the RAF. It didn't work. The next day she was hit by five bombs which put her out of action until at least January.

The optimism of spring 1941 had now become the gloom of summer. Of the seven major ships with which the Kriegsmarine had intended to disrupt the flow of commerce to England, one had been sunk and the remaining six were repairing damage or undergoing refit. For at least two months, until **Admiral Scheer** completed her working up in September, there were no ships available to implement any strategy. Now, with its fortunes at low ebb, SKL was called before Hitler. Ever since the fall of France Hitler had been looking east. And since June 1941 the Army and Luftwaffe had been totally committed to the conquest of Russia. Now his intelligence had come up with some distressing information. Since June Allied counter-intelligence had been spreading rumors that the British were planning an invasion of Norway to aid Russia. Whether Hitler actually believed the story or whether he seized it as an excuse to bring the Kriegsmarine under tighter personal control is not known. But the theme of Russia and Norway came up now and was to dominate Kriegsmarine strategy for the next two years.

The struggle over this change in strategy was to become a test of strength between Raeder and Hitler. Raeder was unshaken in his faith in the Atlantic Strategy, that commerce raiding was the best use for his capital ships. Hitler was skeptical. He had expressed misgivings about the strategy before 'Rheinübung'. Now that **Bismarck** was sunk and Norway apparently threatened, he became increasingly critical. He pointed out the absurdity of the fact that the Kriegsmarine's battleships repeatedly refused battle with enemy capital ships rather than risk damage, yet were put out of action once they reached Brest. Wouldn't the same fate, said Hitler, have befallen **Bismarck** if she had reached port? What good was a fleet poised on the edge of the Atlantic if it couldn't be kept safe. When **Admiral Scheer** became operational at the beginning of September, Hitler for the first time interfered directly with SKL plans. They had wanted **Scheer** to attempt a breakout into the Atlantic to repeat her earlier sortie but Hitler ordered the move delayed. Instead he ordered that she be sent to Oslo as a temporary measure. She was back at Swinemünde within five days however because while at Oslo she came under immediate attack by the RAF, fortunately escaping without being hit. At Swinemünde she joined **Tirpitz** in the Baltic Fleet under the overall command of Vice Admiral Ciliax. It was normal practice for new or repaired units of the fleet to be assigned to the Baltic while working up but both ships were now operational. They remained in the

Admiral Scheer, having finally completed her year-long rebuild, sailed for the Atlantic on 27 October 1940. Before her cruise was completed, she would have been continuously in enemy waters for over five months and would have sunk 17 enemy ships of 113,233GRT and the armed merchant cruiser *HMS Jervis Bay.* One of her victims slips beneath the waves as the crew of one of her 10.5cm flak turrets watches the sport. (Bundesarchiv)

Gneisenau is seen working up in the Baltic in preparation for Operation 'Berlin', the breakout of her and her sister into the Atlantic scheduled for December 1940. Note the black and white recognition stripes that have been superimposed over her camouflage of dark gray bow and stern. These stripes were carried only in the Baltic. They were painted out before any ship sortied into the Atlantic. Ships that wore the recognition stripes also carried carmine (weinrot) turret tops. (Bob Cressman)

During the winter of 1940-41 the Kriegsmarine had its greatest strength deployed in the Atlantic. While *Scheer* was at large in the South Atlantic and the two battleships were raiding in the North Atlantic, *Admiral Hipper* made two sorties from Brest. Here she is seen at that port in January 1941 after arriving from Kiel. Her camouflage of broad dark gray bands over her basic livery was intended to imitate the scheme carried by the battlecruiser *HMS Revenge*. (Bundesarchiv)

Baltic because the situation on land led SKL to believe that the Russian Baltic Fleet might attempt a breakout from the Gulf of Finland. To counter that threat **Tirpitz** and **Scheer** along with **Köln** and **Nurnberg** sortied on 23 September to the Aland Sea between Sweden and Finland. A second group of smaller units around **Emden** operated closer to the shore in support of ground troops. **Tirpitz** and **Scheer** were recalled to Gotenhafen on 24 September, however, when Luftwaffe attacks sank or disabled two Russian battleships and three heavy cruisers (including the **Petropavlovsk**, which, as **Lützow**, had been sold to Russia a year earlier). There the two ships were to remain for three months as the struggle between Hitler and Raeder continued.

When on 13 November 1941 Raeder told Hitler that the three ships at Brest would be ready for action in February, Hitler asked if they could be brought home through the English Channel. Raeder was aghast but said he would look into the feasibility of the idea. When he reported on 29 December that such a move would probably lead to the loss of all ships involved, Hitler responded angrily with a tirade. He claimed that a British invasion of Norway was imminent, that all available ships would shortly be needed there. No time, he said, should be spent on training at Brest. Once the British discovered that they were operational, efforts to disable them would be re-doubled. And he claimed that the long trip around England would be more dangerous than a surprise dash up the Channel. Then he dropped his bombshell. If the plan for the Channel breakthrough wasn't authorized, he would have the ships stricken, taking their guns and crews separately to Norway. Again Raeder was taken aback, begging for a delay before a final decision was made. Finally on 12 January 1942 a grand conference was held at the Wolfschanze in East Prussia. By the end of the day Hitler had his way. Operation 'Cerberus', the Channel Dash, had been approved.

On the evening of 11 February during an air raid alert that neatly hid the departure, **Scharnhorst, Gneisenau** and **Prinz Eugen** slipped out of Brest escorted by six destroyers. The normally efficient RAF radar patrols chose that evening to fail. At dawn the sortie was still undetected. Only at 1042 when they were off Le Havre, were they sighted. Only at 1215, when they were already past, did the Dover batteries open fire, the first British attempt to stop the Germans. All shots missed. Throughout the afternoon British aircraft and motor torpedo boats attacked with an equal lack of success. It was the very secrecy of the preparations for 'Cerberus' which caused the only damage suffered by German ships that day. The inshore channels along the Dutch coast hadn't been swept adequately because to have done so would probably have given the operation away. At 1431 **Scharnhorst** hit a mine which tripped her turbine safety switches, causing her to lose all power. For nearly half an hour she was dead in the water. Later on both **Scharnhorst** and **Gneisenau** hit ground mines for minor damage. Both ships made port on their own steam, **Gneisenau** to Kiel, **Scharnhorst** to Wilhelmshaven. **Prinz Eugen** joined **Admiral Scheer** at Brunsbüttel.

Again, and perhaps for the last time, Hitler proved that the surprise stroke will sometimes succeed against all odds. Logic dictated that Raeder's conclusion should have been correct but boldness upset logic and the breakthrough succeeded with relatively minor damage. 'Cerberus' brought the Atlantic phase of the Kriegsmarine's war to an end. Never again would a German capital ship raid that ocean's shipping lanes. The final postscript came on the night of 26 February. On that night the RAF raided Kiel, hitting **Gneisenau** in the bow with four bombs. Her empty fuel bunkers had yet to be cleaned, leaving them full of explosive vapors. When struck by the bombs the tanks ruptured, gutting her entire forecastle. She was towed to Gotenhafen on 4 April and on 1 July was decommissioned. Plans were made for her conversion to 38cm main armament but little progress was made before all work was stopped in January 1943.

Arriving at Brest at the conclusion of 'Berlin', *Gneisenau* is seen on 22 March 1941. All of the camouflage and stripes she had carried in the Baltic appear to have been painted out. Only at the bow, where wave action wore away the overpainting of medium gray, does the dark gray show through. Note the yellow turret tops and the general deterioration of her paint as the result of months at sea. (Bundesarchiv)

Following on the winter's successes, SKL decided to send its two newest warships, *Bismarck* and *Prinz Eugen*, on an Atlantic raid, 'Rheinübung'. (Above) Seen from *Prinz Eugen*, *Bismarck* is in the standard Baltic scheme; medium gray hull, light gray superstructure, dark gray bow and stern, false bow and stern waves, black and white recognition stripes and carmine turret tops. (NHC) (Left) After a false start in April, 'Rheinübung' commenced on 18 May 1941. Hitler came to Gotenhafen to see the ships off. (Below) This time the British were determined to oppose the breakout. RAF photo-reconnaissance found *Bismarck* at Korsfjord on 21 May 1941. This photo shows her and two oilers at anchor that afternoon. (NHC) (Bottom) *Bismarck* lies off Bergen, 21 May 1941. Part of her crew is over the side on scaffolds painting out the Baltic stripes. Note that her turret tops have already been repainted yellow. (NHC)

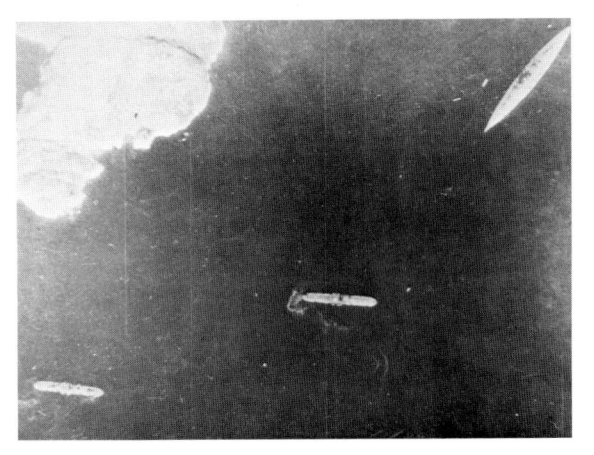

(Above & Right) Because *Bismarck's* radar had failed the previous day, *Prinz Eugen* led the force when *Hood* and *Prince of Wales* were engaged early on 24 May 1941. Initially on *Bismarck's* port bow, *Prinz Eugen* soon crossed over to her disengaged side so as not to mask her guns. The German fire was astoundingly accurate. Seven minutes after opening fire, *Hood* blew up and shortly thereafter *Prince of Wales* was forced to disengage. (NHC)

High Seas Fleet War Badge (Flotten-Kriegsabzeichen)

Among the final German and British photographs of *Bismarck*. (Above) *Bismarck* had been hit only three times in the engagement but one hit in the bow proved to be critical. Her oil tanks were pierced and she began to ship large amounts of water. At dusk on 24 May 1941, Lütjens released *Prinz Eugen* to continue the mission as he turned *Bismarck* toward Brest. As *Prinz Eugen* pulled alongside, final photographs were taken of the wounded giant, showing her noticeably down by the bow. (NHC) (Left) Taken from one of the British destroyers which had shepherded the German battleship through the night of 26-27 May 1941, this photo shows *Bismarck* just before her final engagement.

57

Having sunk *Bismarck* the British set out to neutralize the two battleships which were refitting at Brest. (Above) Under camouflage nets but still readily identifiable, *Scharnhorst* and *Gneisenau* were soon found by RAF reconnaissance. (Right) Soon after being discovered the two were attacked by British bombers. On 10 April RAF Halifaxes put four bombs into *Gneisenau*, effectively nullifying any threat of a renewed raid.

Only five days after taking her leave of *Bismarck, Prinz Eugen* was forced into Brest by the state of her engines. (Below) *Prinz Eugen's* crew marches away from the ship which can be seen lying under nets in drydock. (NHC) (Right) Being refloated, *Prinz Eugen* prepares to leave drydock for the breakthrough back to Germany. (NHC)

Armed merchant cruisers were an effective commerce raiding weapon for the Kriegsmarine. In all nine merchant cruisers sank a total of 136 Allied ships. The most successful, *Schiff 33 (Pinguin)*, sank 32 ships for 154,619GRT before being sunk herself by *HMS Cornwall* off the Seychelles, 8 May 1941. Here one of the cruisers sets out to the cheers of onlookers. She carries a large stencilled American flag as a disguise because the US was still technically neutral at this time and US shipping was rarely interfered with by either side.

In 1941 the U-boat arm suffered some severe setbacks because of improved British ASW methods. The great aces of 1940, Prien, Schepke and Kretschmer were lost in March and in August *U570* surrendered to the Hudson bomber which had damaged her off Iceland. As *HMS Graph* she was an invaluable prize to the British. Reykjavik, 27 August 1941. (Ken Macpherson)

Late 1941 also brought new theaters of operations to Germany's U-boats, the Mediterranean and the US coast, where some great successes were achieved. (Left) *HMS Ark Royal*, perhaps the Royal Navy's most famous aircraft carrier, was sunk by torpedoes from Guggenberger's *U81* off Gibraltar, 13-14 November 1941. (Below Left) Tiesenhuasen's *U331* sank the old battleship *Barham*, also in the Mediterranean, 25 November 1941. (Above) Except for the relatively small number of Type IX boats in service most U-boats couldn't reach the American coast without refuelling. Here a Type VII attempts to catch the fuel line being dragged by a Type XIV 'Milchkuh'. (John Albrecht) (Below) Off the US coast the U-boats found easy pickings as there was neither a blackout nor a convoy system in December 1941. Here a Type IX boat returns to base proudly displaying a flag taken off one of her victims.

Besides the capital ships, which were the most visible, and the U-boats, which were the most successful, the Kriegsmarine depended heavily on smaller forces to do the necessary dirty work around ports and in narrow or shallow waters. (Above) *Richard Beitzen (Z4)* and a torpedo boat are seen at Brest, carrying a splinter camouflage of light and dark gray. (NARS) (Left) A line-up of S-boats can be seen at a French channel port where most S-boats were based. It is obviously maintenance time as the crews of the first two can be seen swabbing the foredecks. (ECPA) (Below Left) Part of a flotilla of R-boats lies berthed together at Lorient. The trident was the flotilla insignia. The center boat carries a rather optimistic sign on its wheelhouse, an arrow pointing to Dover. (ECPA) (Below) To carry out picket duties for which no other boat could be spared, many trawlers were converted into V-boats (Vorpostenboote). Here a V-boat in medium and dark grays is seen off the coast of Norway. (NHC)

Often overlooked because the tonnage involved was tiny in comparison to that of Allied North Atlantic convoys, the Kriegsmarine was also in the business of convoying freighters carrying vital cargoes, particularly off the coast of Norway. (Above) Because the chief danger to coastal convoys was mines, the escorts were frequently M- or R-boats. Here *Brummer* (ex-Norwegian *Olav Tryggvason*) escorts another vessel off Norway. A number of French, Dutch, Danish and Norwegian small craft were pressed into service by the Kriegsmarine. (NHC) (Above Right) This insignia expresses fluently the joys and dangers of minesweeping. (ECPA) (Right) Seen off the fantail of an R-boat, a typical German coastal convoy of four small steamers proceeds up the Norwegian coast. (NHC) (Below) The official Nazi Party line may have condemned and burned much modern art as 'decadent', but the camouflage schemes which were applied to many merchantmen would have warmed an abstract expressionist's heart. 'Decadent' art was alive and well and living in tones of pink, blue, tan, gray and green on the sides of German merchant ships. (ECPA)

When Hitler insisted that the capital ships at Brest be returned to Germany, Raeder fought the idea but lost to the logic of Hitler's arguments and the power of his position. Operation 'Cerberus', the Channel Dash, was just bold enough to work. (Above) *Scharnhorst* follows a half dozen destroyers in the Channel, 12 February 1942. Her upper-works have been given a scruffy coat of dark gray. It has been reported that the ships had light blue turret tops for 'Cerberus'. (Bundesarchiv) (Left) The Luftwaffe gave the Kriegsmarine excellent cooperation for a change on this occasion. A flight of four Bf110s pass over a torpedo boat during 'Cerberus.' (NHC)

Between luck and British complacency, 'Cerberus' caught the defenses napping. (Above) Shell splashes from the Dover batteries appear among the escorts well after that port had been left behind. The fire was at extreme range and inaccurate. (NHC) (Right) Once past Dover, 'Cerberus' had to contend with sporadic air and MTB attacks from the RAF and Royal Navy. Putting on maximum speed, *Scharnhorst* and *Gneisenau* dash for home. (NHC) (Below) Only mines were able to slow the fleet. At 1430 *Scharnhorst* hit a mine which left her dead in the water for a half hour. She is seen from *Prinz Eugen* as she lies stopped. (Bundesarchiv)

Norway,
January 1942 — December 1943

When, in January 1942, **Tirpitz** was transferred from Swinemünde to Trondheim, a new phase of the war began for the Kriegsmarine. As far as Hitler was concerned, **Tirpitz** was there to protect against a planned British invasion though SKL more realistically concluded that such an invasion was unlikely. Perhaps SKL believed that after a while Hitler would get tired of leaving his ships idle in Norwegian waters, that perhaps he would then allow them to resume Atlantic raids from Norwegian bases. For the moment, however, they had to be content to go along with Hitler's order that every available unit be sent to Norway.

On 21 February **Prinz Eugen** and **Admiral Scheer** left Brunsbüttel heading for Trondheim, escorted by three destroyers. The movement was spotted almost immediately by the RAF but the sole bomber that found the force fell victim to **Prinz Eugen's** flak. On 22 February the Germans docked at Grimstadfjord near Bergen, leaving again that night. As they approached Trondheim early the next morning, they were sighted by the submarine **HMS Trident** which put a torpedo into **Prinz Eugen's** stern, almost severing it completely. Fortunately the damage occurred close enough to Trondheim that she was able to be towed in for repairs.

Now Hitler revealed his plans for the ships he was collecting in Norway. He had found a way, he believed, for the Kriegsmarine to 'participate' in the war with Russia that was increasingly filling his thoughts. The surface fleet of the Kriegsmarine would join the U-boats and S-boats in the so far unsuccessful attempt to impede the progress of the PQ convoys to Murmansk, Operation 'Sportpalast'. On 6 March **Tirpitz**, under Vice Admiral Ciliax, escorted by three destroyers, set out after the next convoys, PQ12 and QP8. The sortie was observed by one of the Royal Navy submarines always stationed off Trondheim. **Tirpitz** missed QP8 in the fog on 8 March although one of her escorting destroyers, **Friedrich Ihn (Z14)**, sank a straggler. The next day 12 Albacore torpedo planes off **HMS Victorious** found **Tirpitz** near Vestfjord. The attack failed, two of the Albacores being shot down by **Tirpitz'** flak, but Ciliax didn't need to be reminded that luck with enemy torpedoes went both ways. He turned the force into Vestfjord, docking at Narvik. Three days later **Tirpitz** was back at Trondheim. The first attempt by the major forces which Hitler was collecting in Norway to strangle the Murmansk traffic had been an utter failure.

Following the failure of the raid on PQ12, SKL decided not to risk major units on future sorties unless more definite information existed as to enemy strength and position. SKL hadn't anticipated the speed of the Royal Navy's reaction to **Tirpitz'** sortie. What might have happened had the Albacores been more accurate frightened them very much. Instead, only destroyers would be sent out to challenge PQ13. Another factor in the decision to switch to lighter forces was a newly-felt oil shortage. This problem was brought on by the sudden transfer of the large ships to Norway. The previously adequate tanker traffic from Germany could no longer supply the suddenly increased needs. The problem was to become chronic as Allied bombings of the Rumanian oilfields and the transport routes meant that less and less oil fuel would reach Norway.

On 27 March PQ13 was sighted by a Bv138. The next day ten U-boats and three destroyers of 8. Z-flot. set out from Bergen. On 29 March **Z26** caught and sank a small straggler from the convoy. Then, in turn, amid intermittent snow storms, the three destroyers were intercepted by the cruiser **HMS Trinidad** from the convoy escort. **Trinidad** easily dispatched **Z26** but was hit by one of her own torpedoes, forcing her to withdraw. The remaining two destroyers were able to pick up 96 of **Z26's** crew before they too had to retire. The U-boats managed to sink three more ships from the convoy but lost two of their own number to the escort, making for a less than overwhelming success.

SKL was left in a quandary. The convoys had to be more effectively attacked, but they were reluctant to risk the three operational capital ships now at Trondheim. (**Admiral Hipper** had joined the fleet there in late March after finishing her complete refit. **Prinz Eugen** remained at Trondheim but was in no way operational. She would transfer to Kiel for permanent repairs in May.) To add to the equation, the RAF raided Trondheim on 30 March. No hits were obtained but the point was driven home that ships were not much safer there than they would have been at Brest. SKL was reluctant to move any ships further north because that would only increase the strain on the already tight oil supply. Still the northern ports were very attractive tactically as they would make for a much shorter approach run to the convoys for surface ships. The decision was delayed to await the results of the next battles.

On 8 April PQ14 set out from Iceland, trying a more northerly route. The convoy lost one ship to U-boats before pack ice forced it to turn around. The return convoy, QP10, lost two ships to Ju88s and two more to U-boats. 8. Z-flot. searched for the convoys but missed them both in bad weather. On 29 April the next return convoy, QP11, was sighted by reconnaissance aircraft. On that same day **U456** put two torpedoes into **HMS Edinburgh**, an escorting cruiser. Again three destroyers were sortied to intercept. On 30 April they caught up with the convoy, sinking one ship and damaging another before being chased off by British destroyers. The next day the Germans found the crippled **Edinburgh** which had been straggling behind the convoy. In the ensuing attack, **Hermann Schoemann (Z7)** was sunk by gunfire from **Edinburgh** but **Z24** and **Z25** put another torpedo into the cruiser and sank her. Aircraft and U-boats sank three merchantmen from PQ15 which was passing in the opposite direction.

Obviously SKL was going to have to commit larger units to the convoy

The Kriegsmarine's new strategy was best demonstrated by this RAF reconnaissance photo which shows *Tirpitz* at Trondheim, 12 April 1942. Instead of the Atlantic the Norwegian Sea would be the battleground for the next two years. (NARS)

battles. The destroyers weren't sinking enemy ships and were being lost themselves. On 9 May **Admiral Scheer** was transferred from Trondheim to Narvik and on 24 May was joined by the recently repaired **Lützow**. Now with two heavy cruisers at Narvik and **Hipper** and **Tirpitz** at Trondheim, the Kriegsmarine should have been ready for the next convoy. But, again, Allied counter-intelligence effectively interfered with German plans. False information was fed to the Germans that on 23 May a commando raid would be carried out somewhere on the Norwegian coast. This froze the German fleet in its ports as they awaited the British sortie. Meanwhile, PQ16 sailed for Murmansk. After being sighted on 25 May it was subjected to a massive and co-ordinated air and undersea attack. The Luftwaffe and U-boats combined to sink seven of the convoy's ships. This was a far better showing than any previous attempt and SKL was determined that the next score would be even better.

PQ17 was sighted by reconnaissance on 1 July 1942. (The convoys had been cancelled in June due to the 24-hour daylight at the latitudes at which the convoy battles were being fought.) Operation 'Rösselsprung' was immediately put into effect. On 2 July Group 1 (**Tirpitz** and **Admiral Hipper** with four destroyers) set out from Trondheim, passing up the coastal route to Alta. There it was to be joined by Group 2 (**Admiral Scheer** and **Lützow** with six destroyers) which left Narvik the next day. On that day, however, **Lützow** and three of her accompanying destroyers ran aground in the uncharted waters of the inland passage from Narvik to Alta. The remaining ships gathered at Alta on 4 July, there to await reconnaissance that would pinpoint the enemy covering forces. The British, however, withdrew all their forces from PQ17 when they realized the strength which the Germans had arrayed against them. The four cruisers of the close escort wouldn't have been able to stand against the forces at Alta if they were boldly employed. On 5 July the Admiralty withdrew the escort from PQ17. The 36 merchant ships were dispersed to find their own way to Murmansk.

When the dispersal was reported by aerial reconnaissance, Admiral Schniewind, the new fleet commander, put to sea with **Tirpitz, Scheer, Hipper** and seven destroyers. But no sooner had the task force left the protection of the fjords than the Allies made their presence felt. The Soviet submarine **K-21** made an unsuccessful attack on **Tirpitz** while British aircraft and submarines shadowed the force reporting every move. The reports of the shadowers were intercepted by 'B' Service, which informed SKL. Raeder assumed that the still undetected, and now non-existent, covering forces must have been close and fearing Hitler's wrath should the task force encounter a superior enemy, he recalled Schniewind. The convoy was to be left to the U-boats and aircraft. Between then and 13 July those forces sank 24 of the 36 ships that were trying to make Murmansk. Without any help from the surface fleet a full two-thirds of the convoy had been sunk.

Operation 'Rösselsprung' had been a dismal failure but the attack on PQ17 had succeeded. When PQ18 was sighted on 12 August, no plans were made for interception by surface forces. The convoy was to be attacked by the same combination which had so successfully decimated the previous one. While the results weren't as spectacular, primarily because the convoy wasn't dispersed this time, they were sufficient. 13 out of 39 ships were sunk. This loss rate was unacceptably high for the British. The PQ convoys were cancelled after PQ18. When they were resumed a new name and numbering system was used, so as not to bring up unpleasant memories. The new series began with JW51 when the Murmansk run recommenced in December.

With the deployment of its big ships in Norway a dismal failure up to this point, SKL began to search for a new use for them. They couldn't be risked attacking a convoy as long as their Royal Navy counterparts remained undetected. And now there was an inexplicable lull in the convoys as summer 1942 turned into fall. On 16 August **Admiral Scheer** was sent on Operation 'Wunderland', a commerce raid into the Kara Sea east of Novaya Zemlya. It was a bold foray into previously uncontested waters designed to locate or even shut down the Russian arctic shipping route that sent convoys from the Pacific to Murmansk during the brief summer. **Scheer**, however, found little traffic. On 25 August she caught and sank the icebreaker **Sibiryakov**. The next day she bombarded Port Dikson, the major Soviet arctic port, damaging two merchant ships and doing extensive damage to the docking facilities. By 30 August she was back at Narvik. Between 4 and 8 September the Kriegsmarine again went north. **Richard Beitzen (Z4), Z29** and **Z30** laid mines in the Kara Straits between Novaya Zemlya and the Russian mainland. Again on 24 September a similar operation, 'Zarin', was mounted. This time, **Admiral Hipper** with four destroyers laid a minefield off Novaya Zemlya and returned to Narvik four days later.

At the end of October, at strong Soviet insistence, 13 freighters were allowed to sail independently from Iceland. Five of these were sunk by aircraft and U-boats. On 5 November **Admiral Hipper** and four destroyers were sent against the remaining ships but none were sighted. **Z27** caught and sank a westbound tanker and its escorting sub-chaser. On 15 December, the Allies resumed the Murmansk convoys. The first of the new series, the half-convoy JW51A, reached Russia without incident. Once there, however, three of its ships were lost in a minefield in the White Sea laid in mid-October. The second half of that convoy, JW51B, was sighted from the air on 24 December. The German response was one more surface ship operation. 'Regenbogen' called for **Admiral Hipper** and **Lützow** (**Scheer** had gone to Wilhelmshaven in November, **Lützow** had returned from repairs in early December) escorted by six destroyers to intercept the convoy. To the standing orders to avoid contact with a superior enemy force, SKL now added a restriction to avoid even forces of equal strength. This did nothing to ease the problems of Vice Admiral Kummetz, the force commander. Just as the calm summer weather and long days had earlier favored the Germans, winter now aided the British. Daylight lasted less than two hours per day in late December in the Norwegian Sea. Still Kummetz came up with a clever plan that should have worked. According to the plan, **Hipper** and **Lützow** were to form opposite ends of a sweep line that hopefully would catch the convoy in a crossfire. On 30 December 'Regenbogen' began. First contact was made at 0915 the next day when **Hipper**, the northern half of the pincers, came into contact with the convoy's escorting destroyers. The British reacted by engaging **Hipper** with all available escorts, while routing the convoy southward, away from danger. So far the German plan was working perfectly. **Lützow** should have been just over the horizon speeding toward the unprotected merchantmen. Instead **Lützow's** inexperienced captain continued on a course of due east. At one point she was less than two miles from the convoy which was registering clearly on her radar and was even faintly visible in the mist. Yet **Lützow** remained on a eastward course for another half hour, allowing the convoy to escape behind her. Meanwhile **Hipper** had been busily fighting off the attacks of the British destroyers since 0930. At 1019 she was able to damage **Onslow** but others remained to bar her path. This wouldn't have been critical had **Lützow** been properly commanded but with the convoy free to escape to the south, this tenacious defense saved the day. At 1130 after **Hipper** had disengaged and the two German ships finally found each other, they again came upon the convoy. They quickly sank the destroyer **Achates** and would have made short work of the remaining destroyers had not British luck held that day. At that moment the cruisers **Sheffield** and **Jamaica** came into the action from the north. **Hipper** was quickly hit three times, including a serious hit in No. 3 Boiler and was turning to engage these new antagonists when a further cautionary signal from SKL convinced Kummetz to disengage. During the disengagement the German luck continued bad. **Friedrich Eckoldt (Z16)** mistook the British cruisers for her own ships and was soon sunk by overwhelming gunfire. On New Year's Day 1943 Kummetz docked again at Alta except for **Hipper** which continued on to Kiel for repair of her serious engine damage. Between this hit and the general deterioration of her boilers and engines, **Hipper** would never again be fully operational. At Alta there was no celebration of this very frustrating New Year's.

Hitler had been following the progress of 'Regenbogen' closely and was furious at the outcome. Two German heavy cruisers had had a convoy at their mercy and had let it slip. He went into an immediate tirade to all present ending with the statement that he would scrap the whole surface fleet, putting all resources into U-boats and aircraft. In particular, **Tirpitz, Scharnhorst, Gneisenau, Lützow, Prinz Eugen** and **Admiral Hipper** were to be reduced to scrap immediately. Grand Admiral Raeder felt that he had at last come to the end of his tenure. His arguments no longer carried any weight with Hitler. Ultimately the only influence he had left was in the choice of his successor. He suggested two names: Admiral Rolf Carls of Gruppe Nord or Admiral Karl Dönitz, BdU (Befehlshaber der U-boote – Commander of U-boats). Not surprisingly Hitler chose Dönitz because U-boats were undoubtedly the most important element of the Kriegsmarine strategically and also because Hitler felt certain that Dönitz would readily agree with his plans to scrap the surface fleet. If so he was in for a surprise.

On 23 January 1943 a 'Fuhrerbefehl' ordered the paying off of all major fleet units not needed for training duties. He had every expectation that his new Grand Admiral would follow orders. Dönitz was promoted to his new rank on 30 January, making his first report to Hitler on 8 February. At that time Dönitz submitted to a surprised Hitler a revised plan that called for paying off only **Gneisenau, Hipper, Leipzig** and **Köln**. The first two were already in a decommissioned state undergoing lengthy repairs, the latter two were old light cruisers which hadn't seen active service since 1941. That was as far as Dönitz was willing to go. To Hitler's surprise he took the position that the continued existence of the battlefleet was necessary. If it was scrapped, he said, the British would be free to release their escort vessels for anti-submarine warfare.

At the completion of 'Cerberus' *Prinz Eugen* joined *Admiral Scheer* at Brunsbüttel. (Top) *Prinz Eugen* as she looked in late February 1942. Her hull still shows traces of the stripes she carried in the Baltic a year earlier. (Bundesarchiv) (Above) *Scheer* seen from *Prinz Eugen* as the two sailed for Norway on 21 February 1942. (NHC) (Left) Two days later *Prinz Eugen* was torpedoed by *HMS Trident* nearly losing her stern, putting her out of service for 11 months. Because no major repair facilities existed at Trondheim, repair ships had to be brought in to assist in the work of cutting away her damaged fantail. (NARS) (Below) With her stern blanked off and two emergency rudders fitted, *Prinz Eugen* sailed for Kiel on 16 May 1942. (NHC)

One of the 'four-pipers' traded to England in September 1940, *HMS Campbeltown* ended her life in glorious fashion. In order to deny the Germans the use of the drydock at St-Nazaire, the only dock in France large enough to handle *Tirpitz*, she was loaded with explosives and rammed into the dock gates, 28 March 1942. A few moments after this photo was taken, she blew up, taking the dock gates and many curious Germans with her. (Bundesarchiv)

The attempt to intercept PQ13 in March 1942 was restricted to three destroyers by the worsening oil shortage. One of the attackers, *Z26,* came up against *HMS Trinidad* and definitely got the worse of the engagement.

All these operations had . . . primarily during the later stages of the war, the object of keeping the English Fleet busy and preventing it, by immobilizing parts of the fleet, from being able to concentrate on the formation of more vigorous U-boat defenses, as had been the case at the end of the last war.

Dönitz intended to keep the fleet. **Admiral Scheer** and **Prinz Eugen** were to be assigned to training duties. **Tirpitz, Scharnhorst** and **Lützow** were to remain in Norway.

Hitler now was the one who needed time to think. But when the two met next on 26 February, Dönitz was insistent. He demanded that the now-repaired **Scharnhorst** be sent to join **Tirpitz** and **Lützow** at Alta.

Unused to such resolute resistance from the Kriegsmarine, Hitler gave in. On 8 March **Scharnhorst** set off on the long dash to Alta.

While the surface units in Norway had been virtually immobilized as their fate was being decided, the JW convoys hadn't stopped. The next two got through with only minor losses but when **Scharnhorst** joined the fleet at Alta, the concentration of power there caused the Royal Navy to cancel the remaining convoys scheduled for that spring and summer, which in turn led to exactly the consequence that Dönitz had hoped to avoid by keeping the surface fleet afloat. The British withdrew the escorts assigned to the Murmansk run and threw them into the Battle of the Atlantic at a critical time. March and April 1943 had been record months for Dönitz' U-boats but in May the addition of the extra escorts along with recently introduced very long range aircraft and the first of the 'jeep' carriers combined to swing the tide dramatically in the Allies' favor. By 25 May the defense had become so intense that Dönitz was

67

obliged to withdraw his boats from the Atlantic. This was a turning point far less spectacular but far more crucial than the loss of **Bismarck**. Never again did the more sober minds at SKL think about winning at sea. Perhaps the time had come "to show that they could die with dignity".

Between the lack of convoys and the lack of oil, the remainder of the spring and summer were relatively quiet in Norway. Early in July and again later in the month, combined USN-Royal Navy forces demonstrated off Norway to divert German attention from the invasion of Sicily and possibly draw the Kriegsmarine into battle. The Allied fleet was never even sighted, however, so the ploy came to nothing. On 1 August Operation 'Wunderland II' was initiated, similar to 'Wunderland' of the preceeding year. This time **Lützow** was to do the raiding but, since **Scheer** had found so few targets on her sortie, the decision was made to reconnoiter the area from the air before **Lützow** sailed. Accordingly, **U255** set up a fuel dump and supply base on Novaya Zemlya from which a Bv138 flying boat conducted four reconnaissance flights as far east as the Vilkitski Straits (the same East Latitude as Singapore) but not enough worthwhile targets were found and the operation was cancelled.

In response to rumors that Spitsbergen's bays were being used as shelter by stragglers from the JW convoys, and perhaps a little desperate to find some suitable employment for their remaining big ships, SKL approved Operation 'Sizilien' (Or 'Zitronella'). The plan called for **Tirpitz** and **Scharnhorst** to bombard any inhabited areas of Spitsbergen, to search out any Allied shipping and to land troops to establish watch and supply stations. Leaving Alta on 6 September with an escort of nine destroyers, two days later **Scharnhorst** landed troops at Gronfjord and Advent Bay while **Tirpitz** bombarded Barentsburg. By 9 September all ships were safely back at Alta, having found no trace of enemy shipping. In truth few Allied ships had used Spitsbergen for refuge up to that point but the German raid got the Allies interested. On 19 October the cruiser **USS Tuscaloosa** escorted by four destroyers landed troops to set up Allied bases there.

The presence of such a large concentration of German strength beyond the effective reach of land-based airpower continued to mesmerize British planners. A number of novel, and often bizarre, plans for attacking the giants at Alta were proposed before Operation 'Source' was approved. On 21 September six regular Royal Navy submarines towed six X-craft midget submarines to the mouth of Altafjord and cast them off. Of the six X-craft four were lost or disabled but, incredibly, X6 and X7 managed to survive the tricky currents, uncharted rocks, minefields and nets to plant their charges under **Tirpitz'** keel. The resulting detonations left **Tirpitz** unmaneuverable, facing six months of repairs. Fearing a repetition of the attack **Lützow** left for the Baltic on 23 September, reaching Gotenhafen on 1 October 1943.

With **Tirpitz** out of action and **Lützow** in the Baltic only **Scharnhorst** remained as an active threat in the Arctic. The British felt sufficiently confident of their ability to handle a single battleship to resume the JW convoys on 15 November with JW54A. Both halves of JW54 were able to get through without being sighted and suffered no losses. On 19 December Dönitz informed Hitler of his intention to send **Scharnhorst** out to challenge the next convoy. Three days later JW55B was sighted. Close escort for the convoy was provided by eight destroyers, middle cover by three heavy cruisers and distant cover by the battleship **HMS Duke of York**, the heavy cruiser **HMS Jamaica** and four destroyers. On Christmas day, unaware of **Duke of York's** location, SKL authorized Operation 'Ostfront'. **Scharnhorst** and five destroyers, under Rear Admiral "Achmed" Bey, set out in the teeth of a full-fledged arctic gale. The next morning found the German ships spread in a sweepline, searching for the convoy in the brief twilight. At 0926 the three cruisers of the middle cover found **Scharnhorst** on their radars and began a rapid and accurate fire. The German battleship hadn't been using her radar and was taken completely by surprise. Throughout the war SKL had refused to accept the notion that British HF/DF was pinpointing the location of German ships. The only explanation SKL could imagine for the uncanny ability of the British to find their ships in open water was that German radars were giving off radiations on which the British were homing. This conviction led to the self-defeating practice, as was the case with **Scharnhorst,** of not turning on the radar set until the target had been found visually. In the arctic in December against radar-equipped adversaries this was suicidal. In as many minutes **Norfolk** obtained two 8″ hits on **Scharnhorst,** one of which destroyed the radar that had just been turned on. Unable to see the enemy which was damaging her, **Scharnhorst** was forced to disengage. After releasing his destroyers to search for the convoy on their own, Bey turned **Scharnhorst** again in pursuit of the convoy. At 1224 she again encountered the heavy cruisers. In the somewhat better visibility that then obtained, she was able to register two 28cm hits on her previous tormentor, **Norfolk,** but fearing that they might have been screening for a British battleship, Bey again retired. Having now tried twice to find the convoy and having on each occasion been blocked by cruisers, Bey considered his duty to be done and turned **Scharnhorst** toward Alta. She never made port. At 1617 the distant cover force, which had all day been steaming up from the west at high speed, found **Scharnhorst** on radar at a range of 23 miles. At 1656 **Duke of York** engaged **Scharnhorst,** obtaining several 14″ hits but the latter's superior speed enabled her to pull away. After an hour's chase, however, **Duke of York's** escorting destroyers in a well executed attack put four torpedoes into **Scharnhorst,** bringing her to a halt. Then the end was inevitable. Battered by innumerable hits from **Duke of York's** guns and an additional ten or eleven torpedoes, **Scharnhorst** sank at 1945, only 36 survivors being picked up out of the frigid waters.

Scharnhorst's loss can be blamed on a variety of reasons, all of which had been factors in the overall failure of the German naval offensive. The poor planning, the inadequate or non-existent aerial reconnaissance and the over-restrictive orders from SKL all played their part. But again on this occasion, as had happened so many times before, it was lack of communication between the Luftwaffe and the Kriegsmarine which doomed **Scharnhorst**. The one piece of information which could have saved Admiral Bey was timely word about the presence or location of British capital ships. While the presence of **Duke of York** had been suspected by German intelligence, there wasn't enough solid information to assist Bey. But at 1012 on 26 December a radar-equipped Bv138 reported contact with major ships heading in the direction of **Scharnhorst,** approximately 150 miles west of her position. Again at 1140 the plane reported the contacts as being one large and several small ships. Incredibly the first report wasn't passed along to Bey until 1306. By the time it had been deciphered and delivered, the information was already four hours old and **Scharnhorst** was already doomed. Had the information reached Bey when it could have, at least two hours sooner, it might have been soon enough. Sadly, after four years of war, the loss of yet another warship could be blamed on the fact that no effective communication had been set up between two supposedly co-operating arms of service.

With the loss of **Scharnhorst,** the offensive against the Murmansk convoys effectively came to an end. Only a much reduced force of U-boats and aircraft continued to attempt to hinder that traffic with decreasing success. Never again would the ability of the Allies to move ships on the sea be seriously challenged by the Kriegsmarine. Of the power that the Kriegsmarine had poised on the convoy route, now only the damaged **Tirpitz** remained. In March 1944 she again came to the attention of the British. Much to their surprise she was again in service. Having been repaired *in situ*, she was now working up, undergoing mechanical trials. On 3 April the Royal Navy launched Operation 'Tungsten'. The aircraft carriers **Furious** and **Victorious** sent 41 Barracudas to Alta, obtaining 14 bomb hits which put **Tirpitz** out of action for another three months. Carrier strikes were attempted again in late April and May but without further success. By July **Tirpitz** was again able to move and was transferred from Alta to a more defensible position in nearby Kaafjord. On 17 July, 45 Barracudas were launched from **Formidable, Indefatigable** and **Furious** but the effective smoke and flak defense at the new anchorage prevented any hits. Twice more the same ships launched similar attacks but only two minor hits were obtained. The realization dawned at the Admiralty that carrier-borne aircraft weren't going to succeed in sinking **Tirpitz**.

A change in tactics was needed. If only a few hits could be obtained, then they alone had to be enough. The RAF suggested using the 5.4 ton 'Tallboy' bomb which had been developed for use against reinforced concrete bunkers. On 15 September, 28 Lancasters, each loaded with a single 'Tallboy', flew from North Russian bases against Kaafjord. Only a single hit on **Tirpitz'** bow was obtained but enough were near misses to again leave her unmaneuverable. On 17 October she was towed to Tromsö and docked in water thought to be too shallow for her to be sunk. The hope was that if she sank, she would remain upright and her guns would remain usable. 32 Lancasters attacked her there on 29 October without result and again on 12 November she was attacked by 21 heavy bombers. On this latter occasion three hits were obtained. At last it was enough. **Tirpitz** capsized and settled on the bottom on her side. While the end of the presence of German capital ships in Norway effectively came with the sinking of **Scharnhorst,** the last chapter wasn't written until 11 months later with the loss of **Tirpitz.**

As destroyers had been ineffective in slowing the Murmansk traffic, SKL decided to contest PQ17 with all forces at hand. *Tirpitz* (Right) and *Admiral Hipper* (Below) were at Trondheim. Both carried an elaborate dark gray splinter pattern. (NHC) (Bottom) Meanwhile, *Lützow* and *Admiral Scheer* were based at Narvik. Here *Lützow* is seen wearing a similar splinter scheme. (NHC)

The German response to PQ17 was an elaborate plan, Operation 'Rösselsprung', involving all four major vessels in Norway. (Left) The convoy was first sighted by the Luftwaffe on 4 July 1942. It is seen here before its dispersal later on the same day. (NHC) (Below) Group 2 of 'Rösselsprung', *Tirpitz* and *Admiral Hipper* with four destroyers, was ordered from Trondheim to Alta on 2 July 1942. Here *Hipper* and two destroyers are seen from *Tirpitz*. (NHC) (Bottom) Minus *Lützow* and three destroyers which ran aground, Group 2 (*Admiral Scheer* and four destroyers) reached Alta on 4 July 1942. The entire force sortied the next day. *Hipper*, *Scheer* and five destroyers are visible from *Tirpitz* in this view. (NHC)

After the fiasco of 'Rösselsprung', SKL felt compelled to find a use for the vessels now at Alta. Operation 'Wunderland' sent *Admiral Scheer* into the Kara Sea. (Above) The Soviet icebreaker *Sibiryakov* was caught and sunk, 25 August 1942. (NHC) (Left) The crew of the sinking icebreaker was taken off by *Scheer's* boats. (NHC) (Below) The next evening, *Scheer* bombarded Port Dikson, the main Soviet Arctic port at the mouth of the Yenisey River, damaging two ships. (NHC)

Late 1942 saw the beginning of the offensive that would defeat the U-boats in the Atlantic. (Above) One element that led to the Allied victory was the great increase in surface escorts, enough so that 'Hunter-Killer Groups' could be formed. Part of such a group, *USCG Spencer* got *U175* when she was forced to the surface on 17 April 1943. (NARS) (Right) Most important was the ability of the Allies to provide air cover over the entire ocean. No longer was surface action safe. Surface resupply operations were particularly vulnerable. Here one of a pair of boats caught on the surface disappears in the explosion of an aerial depth charge. (NARS)

The only force that could have changed the outcome of the Battle of the Atlantic would have been a carrier-borne naval air force. Work on the aircraft carrier *Graf Zeppelin* was resumed for seven months late in 1942. The hull of the fifth heavy cruiser, *Seydlitz,* on which no progress had been made since her launch in January 1939, was taken in hand for conversion. Seen here at Bremen on 3 February 1943, *Seydlitz* was eventually scuttled incomplete at Königsberg in April 1945. (Ken Macpherson)

A small measure of revenge came on 29 May 1944 when the escort carrier *USS Block Island* was sunk by *U549* but the ability of the Allies to give 24-hour aircraft protection to convoys turned the tide decisively in the Atlantic. (NARS)

The men who led and lost the naval war; on the left Grand Admiral Raeder, next to him the man who replaced him in January 1943 Admiral Dönitz and Hitler, who increasingly restricted the use of his ships after the loss of *Bismarck,* to the point that they were rendered impotent.

Dönitz maintained that the large ships had to be kept, if only to ease pressure on his U-boats. In one of the rare operations during these months, 'Sizilien' was mounted in September 1943. (Right) *Scharnhorst* landed troops on Spitsbergen, 8 September 1943. Note a faintly visible camouflage scheme, light gray bow and stern, dark gray center. (NHC) (Below) At the same time, *Tirpitz* shelled Barentsburg. She is now carrying a somewhat less complex dark gray splinter camouflage. (NHC)

Soon after 'Sizilien', on 21 September 1943, *Tirpitz* was seriously damaged by mines laid by two British X-craft. She never again saw offensive action. (Above) While lying at Alta, her turrets and guns were canvas covered and her deck often strewn with fresh-cut pine trees. (NHC) (Left) Part of *Tirpitz'* crew watches a pair of rather limber dancers perform their act. (NHC) (Below) *Tirpitz* had been repaired when she was again damaged, this time by naval aircraft. During this period, her deck was camouflaged with dark shapes (reportedly green and brown). Note the oil leaks. (Bottom) She was finally towed to Tromsö in October 1944. There she was twice attacked by RAF Lancasters and finally sunk on 12 November 1944.

The only light cruiser to remain relatively undamaged in the early stages of the war, *Köln* spent her time as a training vessel in the Baltic. She wears the now nearly standard dark gray splinter camouflage. Like most other Kriegsmarine warships in the Baltic, *Köln* would again see action in the final days.

The End,
January 1944 — May 1945

By the end of 1943 the surface units of the Kriegsmarine had been largely neutralized by Allied air and sea power. Even the U-boats were only marking time in the Atlantic, waiting for the arrival of the revolutionary Type XXI and XXIII boats. What major ships still remained (**Prinz Eugen, Admiral Hipper, Admiral Scheer, Lützow** and the three light cruisers) were being used to train sailors for a future battlefleet for which hope was rapidly fading. Only the more foolish or stubborn, such as Dönitz, saw any reason or hope in the continued struggle.

Serious as the situation was, there were still grounds which encouraged the hope of a last-minute turn of the tide. The fighter program with its new types... promised the possiblity of checking or even putting an end to the enemy's uncontrolled air supremacy over the whole German area. The new types of U-boats led to the expectation of a powerful impetus to U-boat warfare. Therefore the leaders' task was to hold out and concentrate all forces in the most important tasks until the new weapons could be brought into operation.

For most, the months that remained were an exercise in discipline, honor and pride. Only in the Baltic was there a 'positive' object to be gained from continued activity, the rescuing of thousands of refugees from the advancing Russians.

During this period the small forces came to be probably the most important element of the Kriegsmarine. When the Allies brought the relatively quiet early months of 1944 to an end with the Normandy invasion in June, the only forces besides U-boats available to resist were the small forces: destroyers, torpedo boats, S-boats, R-boats and the miscellaneous small minelayers and sweepers, patrol and picket boats and sub chasers which had been doing the dirty work all along. There was also one new addition to the small forces, the K-Verbände (Kleinkampf-Verbände – Small Weapons Groups). These included a whole range of one- and two-man U-boats, piloted torpedoes and explosive speedboats. They were the weapons of desperation. This type of weapon had been used by other nations earlier in the war. The Italians had used their 'Chariots' with success in the Mediterranean and the British X-craft had immobilized **Tirpitz**. Theoretically these weren't suicide craft such as would be employed by the Japanese a year later. Provision was always made for the crew to survive and sometimes even return to base. But the very size and vulnerability of these weapons made them extremely dangerous. The odds were always against the crew's survival. For example, the first time that the K-Verbände took offensive action was on 20 April 1944 when 37 Neger one-man torpedoes were sent against the landings at Anzio. No successes were obtained and only 13 of the Neger-pilots returned to try again.

The forces that the Allies arrayed for 'Overlord', the Normandy Invasion, were overwhelming. Seven battleships, two monitors, 23 cruisers, three gunboats, 105 destroyers and 1073 landing craft could be opposed by a total German force on the French coast of five destroyers, six torpedo boats and 34 S-boats. Still the Kriegsmarine counterattacked as best it could. Attempting to reach the landing craft, 5. T-flot. (**Möwe, Falke, Jaguar** and **T28**) sortied from Le Havre on the night of 6 June.

In Gotenhafen, probably in early 1944, *Lützow* is seen as she appeared after refit following her return from Norway in September 1943. She wears a coat of overall dark gray. (Ken Macpherson)

Allied tactical airpower made the coast of France an unhealthy place for German shipping of all types. (Above) *T24* and *Z24* are seen from a strafing aircraft. Those ships which weren't sunk were forced to retreat back to home waters. (Below) Between 24 and 26 August 1944 the remaining German naval power in France was decimated by a series of RAF Mosquito raids on Bordeaux and the Gironde.

They never got close but they did manage to sink a Norwegian destroyer before superior firepower forced them to withdraw. The landings were in no way impeded. The next night 5. S-flot (10 S-boats) joined the attack, sinking an LST and an LCT but losing two of their own to mines. During the day on 8 June, 8. Z-flot (**Z24, Z32, ZH1** and **T24**) sailed from Brest, hoping to reach the beaches from the south. They were intercepted, however, by the Royal Navy's 10th Destroyer Flotilla (8 destroyers) and completely overwhelmed. **ZH1** went down almost immediately because of a torpedo from **HMS Ashanti**. **Z32** was driven ashore and blown up. One British destroyer was damaged.

On succeeding evenings the Kriegsmarine threw in all available forces in a desperate attempt to influence the course of events on land. Over the course of the next month the Germans succeeded in sinking four steamers, one motor torpedo boat, one motor gunboat, one tug and an LST while losing six S-boats and one R-boat. On the night of 14 June the RAF reacted to this harrassment. 325 Lancasters hit the dock area at Le Havre, sinking **Falke, Jaguar** and **Möwe,** 14 S-boats, seven R-boats and eight picket boats. This effectively broke the back of the nocturnal offensive against the Normandy beachhead, though the attacks would continue with declining regularity and results until the French ports fell to the advancing Allies.

A few K-Verbände attacks were attempted but with disappointing results, mainly due to the extreme range at which these weapons were being employed. On the evening of 5 July Negers were employed against the beachhead for the first time. They were based at Villers-sur-Mer, east of Caen. The attacks that night sank two minesweepers. Attacking again two nights later, another minesweeper and an MTB were sunk and the Polish destroyer **Dragon** seriously damaged. The greatest success by the Negers was the sinking of the destroyer **HMS Isis** on 20 July. The attacks began to diminish soon, however, due to a shortage of Negers. The last attack was launched on 17 August. The results were typical. Two small Allied steamers were sunk but only 16 out of 42 Negers returned. On 2 August, 20 Linse explosive motorboats of 211. K-flot. sank the destroyer **HMS Quorn** and a trawler.

The slow but steady advance of the British land forces east of Caen gradually forced the remaining K-Verbände out of range of the Normandy beaches. Soon thereafter Patton's US Third Army broke through at St-Lô, dooming the German Forces in France on sea as well as land. At the same time that the Allies were surrounding the French ports on the land side, the Royal Navy and RAF launched sweeps to clear the Bay of Biscay. As German ships attempted to flee the trap, many were caught and sunk by the British. On 21 August, **Z23** was caught by British aircraft off La Pallice and sunk. Likewise **Z24** and **T24** were caught off Le Verdon at the mouth of the Gironde in the evening on 24 August. The next evening RAF Mosquitoes hit Bordeaux, sinking **Z37**, four R-boats, two auxilliary minesweepers, two picket boats and 21 merchant ships. France had become a killing ground for the Kriegsmarine.

With the loss of France, only Norway and the Baltic remained as theaters of action for the Kriegsmarine. Norway now served as the last base for Dönitz' U-boats. There the new Type XXIs were to be based which, it was hoped, would swing the Battle of the Atlantic back again to the Germans. But for the moment and for many months to come the old boats, the Type VIIs and IXs, still sailed against the Allies despite the tremendous odds they faced. Only in the Baltic were there the ships and the relative freedom of movement for the surface fleet of the Kriegsmarine to prove still useful.

As the Russians advanced along the Baltic coast, after breaking out from the encirclement of Leningrad, the Kriegsmarine found opportunities to support the retreating German armies. In June 1944 the 2nd Task Force was formed in the Baltic composed of **Prinz Eugen, Lützow** and 6. Z-flot. (The 1st TF still technically existed around **Tirpitz** in Norway.) The composition of this force varied throughout the remainder of the war but its task remained constant: the support of ground troops. On 20 August the 2nd Task Force engaged in its first action when **Prinz Eugen** shelled Russian troop concentrations near Tukums, west of Riga on the Gulf of Riga. Between 17 and 23 September the small forces of the task force lifted 50,000 troops and 85,000 civilian refugees from the Estonian Pocket. Again between 6 and 10 October **Prinz Eugen** and **Lützow** were employed against a Russian breakthrough between Memel and Libau. Five days later **Prinz Eugen** rammed **Leipzig** while the two ships were maneuvering in the fog off the coast near Memel. The damage to **Leipzig** was serious, that to **Prinz Eugen** relatively minor. She was back in action in a month.

A battle had been raging throughout October on the Baltic island of Ösel at the entrance to the Gulf of Riga. By the end of the month the German defenders had been pushed back onto the narrow Sword Peninsula. A Russian attack on Swörbe on 22 October was beaten back by shelling from **Lützow**. On 20 November **Prinz Eugen** was back in action also supporting positions on Swörbe. Two days later **Admiral Scheer** replaced **Prinz Eugen,** continuing to support the defenders there until they were forced to evacuate the next morning.

There was a lull after the battle of Ösel ended. Except for the loss of **Z35** and **Z36** in a minefield on 12 December, most German ships saw little action in December and January. Only when new Russian attacks between Königsberg and Pillau threatened to cut the retreat of major German forces in Lithuania and East Prussia was the 2nd Task Force again called into action. On 29 and 30 January 1945 **Prinz Eugen** supported a German attack from Cranz (Samland) toward Fischhausen on the Frisches Haff. The attack failed. On 8 February **Lützow** supported units of 4. Armee near Frauenberg between Königsberg and Elbing. For the next two days **Scheer** joined her sister. A new German attack at Fischhausen on 18 February was supported by **Admiral Scheer** outside and smaller forces inside the Frisches Haff. This time the attack succeeded. The escape route to Pillau was restored and the evacuation from the east continued. It was to be the greatest lift of human beings by water in history. For example, on the first three days after the route to Pillau was reopened, over 62,000 troops and civilians were evacuated. While engaged in this activity, **Z28** was lost to mining off Sassnitz on 6 March.

By 9 March **Admiral Scheer** was shelling Russian positions in support of the Wollin bridgehead at the mouth of the Oder, hardly 100 miles from Berlin. The end was obviously in sight. The only reason now to continue the fight, from the Kriegsmarine's point of view, was that each day meant more refugees could be saved from the oncoming Soviets. So they kept up the fight, knowing that each small victory only delayed the inevitable. On 10 March the Russians broke through again in East Prussia. On that day **Prinz Eugen** joined in the battle to hold onto the port of Gotenhafen. From 15 through 21 March the old battleship **Schlesien** replaced **Prinz Eugen** and was then replaced herself by **Lützow**. On 25 March even **Leipzig**, immobilized at the dock at Gotenhafen since her ramming, joined in the bombardment. On 27 March the decommissioned hulk of **Gneisenau** was towed out to the harbor entrance and sunk as a blockship. Three days later, **Köln** was sunk by USAAF heavy bombers in Wilhelmshaven. Operation 'Walpurgisnacht', the evacuation of over 38,000 refugees who had gathered on the Hela Peninsula, was carried out on the evening of 4 April, covered by **Lützow** and three destroyers.

Now, at last, the lack of fuel oil and ammunition and the miserable state of repair of ships which had been fighting without refit for too long caused SKL to order the withdrawal of the remaining heavy ships. One by one they came back from the east to be sunk or scuttled or surrendered. On 9 April **Prinz Eugen** and **Lützow** transferred to Swinemünde. On the same day **Admiral Scheer** and **Admiral Hipper** arrived at Kiel. There both ships were hit by an RAF raid, **Scheer** capsizing beside her dock. On 16 April the RAF bombed Swinemünde with 'Tallboy' bombs. **Lützow** settled on the bottom in an upright position. Her guns were still serviceable and were used in several defensive actions until the ammunition gave out. The still incomplete aircraft carrier **Graf Zeppelin** was scuttled at Stettin on 25 April. On 2 May **Schlesien** was on her way to the Greifwalder Bodden to protect the Wolgast Bridgehead but she struck a mine and was forced to return to Swinemünde. The oldest ship in the fleet had been sent on the Kriegsmarine's last offensive operation and had failed.

The end now came swiftly. On 3 May **Admiral Hipper** was scuttled north of Kiel. The next day the remains of **Lützow** and **Schlesien** were blown up to keep them out of Russian hands. **Prinz Eugen** and **Nurnburg** proceded to Copenhagen, where they surrendered to the British on 8 May 1945. In the last Kriegsmarine operation of the war (it actually took place after the armistice had technically begun) five destroyers and four torpedo boats lifted 20,000 final refugees from Hela on the morning of 8 May. In retrospect, most Kriegsmarine veterans believe that this evacuation of refugees was the most important task, with the possible exception of the U-boat offensive, which the Kriegsmarine undertook. In all, 1,420,000 refugees were lifted from the Gulf of Danzig and Pomerania to safer havens in the west.

Yet compared to the millions more who couldn't be evacuated, who are now in East Germany, Poland and Russia, that figure was a drop in the proverbial bucket. The Kriegsmarine had been too small when the war began and was too small when it ended. Its victories had been glorious but couldn't tip the scales of 'Weltpolitik' in Germany's favor. Only in the commerce war was the Kriegsmarine able to threaten England. Yet this had been totally unforeseen in SKL's prewar planning. When the time was ripe for England to be strangled in 1940-41, the means simply weren't there. If the U-boats that were rolling off the ways in 1943 had been available two years before, if all German warships had been designed with commerce raiding in mind, if SKL had known that war would come in 1939, if SKL had appreciated fully the threat of airpower, if Hitler had been less restrictive in the use of his ships after the loss of **Bismarck** then, perhaps, the result might have been different. But the fact remains that the Kriegsmarine had been too small, composed of the wrong ships and planned and directed in an often unrealistic manner. Still, with all its obvious problems, the Kriegsmarine had been able to make the very survival of England problematical for several years. It was ironic that the arm of service that interested Hitler least was the only one that could have defeated England and decisively tilted the war against Russia. Again, history showed that the nation which doesn't appreciate the uses of the seas and seapower will lose its wars.

The only sustained use of the K-Verbände was on the French coast following the Normandy Invasion. (Above Right) A dozen Linse explosive boats prepare to leave harbor for the major attack on 2 August 1944 in which a British destroyer was sunk. (Right) Four Biber two-man subs can be made out among the V-boats and trawlers in this small French port. The Biber was never perfected to the point that it was able to seriously threaten Allied shipping. (Below Left) A Kampfschwimmer displays his diving watch to Grand Admiral Dönitz. (Below Right) The most successful, at least in number deployed, of the craft used by the K-Verbände were the Neger one-man torpedoes. Here the plexiglas dome is being lowered over the head of the pilot. His bravery can't be doubted even if his intelligence can, as only about one-third of the Negers returned from any mission.

The task of which the Kriegsmarine was the proudest in the last days was the rescuing of refugees from East Prussia. (Left) Masses of civilians fled the encircling Russian armies, fearing vengeance for some of the German practices in that country. (Above) Similarly any military units that could be rescued from the east were desperately needed behind the Oder.

Combat Badge of the Small Battle Units
(Kampfabzeichen der Kleinkampfmittel)

While smaller units were lifting refugees, what major warships remained still operable were employed in shore bombardment. *Admiral Hipper* (Left) and *Köln* (Below) both supported the troops ashore. *Hipper* was still suffering from severe boiler problems which kept her in port much of the time. (NHC)

During complex off-shore maneuvering, *Prinz Eugen* rammed *Leipzig* in the fog off Danzig, 15 October 1944. (Above) The two ships were locked together for several hours until they could be safely separated. (NHC) (Above Right) *Prinz Eugen's* bow plating was peeled back by the impact for a considerable distance. (Right) *Leipzig* was towed into Gotenhafen, where she remained while being repaired. While at the dock she added the force of her guns to the defense of the city.

The last evacuation from Libau was on SAT (Schwere Artillerie Träger — heavy gunboat) *Nienburg*. These evacuations continued up to and even beyond the surrender. In all over 1,400,000 refugees were rescued from East Prussia and Pomerania.

79

Inevitably many ships which had fought bravely came to sad ends. (Left) Still missing her bow, *Gneisenau* was sunk as a blockship at the entrance to Gotenhafen, 27 March 1945 (Bob Cressman) (Below Left) The pre-dreadnought *Schlesien* saw some major action in the final bombardments. She was on her way to another such when she ran into mines in the Greifwalder Bodden. She was eventually scuttled at Swinemünde, 4 May 1945. (Below) *Köln* was sunk by USAAF bombers at Wilhelmshaven, 30 March 1945. (Public Archives Canada)

After being scuttled at Stettin on 25 April 1945, the still incomplete *Graf Zeppelin* was refloated by the Russians in September of that year. Some thought was given to her completion but in the end no further work was done on her. She eventually succumbed to a mine two years later. *Prinz Eugen* became an atomic guinea pig, and several U-boats and destroyers went to Allied navies as reparations but most were scrapped within a few years. Only *Nurnberg*, which became the Russian *Admiral Makarov*, continued to soldier on for years to come. (NHC)

80